HARVEST
Home

*American Settlers Gather
the Harvest in Four
Inspiring Novellas*

Janet Lee Barton
Ellen Edwards Kennedy
Debby Mayne
Janet Spaeth

BARBOUR
PUBLISHING, INC.
Uhrichsville, Ohio

Harvest of Love by Janet Lee Barton
It was unthinkable for Liddy Evans to suddenly find herself widowed, pregnant, and the object of a ruthless banker's attention. Liddy needs some protection and help with her alfalfa harvest. Calvin McAllister needs someone to teach his young daughters the art of being ladies. It is a convenient trade of services, but then why does it get harder to part each evening?

The Applesauce War by Ellen Edwards Kennedy
In a mischievous attempt to match their children together, Verity McCracken's and Pete Delorme's fathers have created a real rift between the families. The McCrackens need help to harvest their bountiful apple crop, but the Delormes won't lend one hand this year. Verity and Pete work together to try and decipher how the problem ever started between Christians, but that only makes the fathers madder. How can this rotten feud be mended?

Sunshine Harvest by Debby Mayne
What is a young woman to do when her father suddenly dies, her mother goes into depression, and a large crew of citrus harvesters are depending on her for their livelihood? Anna Drake is not a quitter and she won't accept charity. But Daniel Hopkins is not deterred from showing Christian kindness, and soon Anna is surrendering segments of her stubborn heart.

Only Believe by Janet Spaeth
Catherine's brother raised her after their parents' death; now it is her turn to help him. As he lies in a Minnesota hospital, Catherine goes to his Dakota homestead and prepares to bring in the wheat harvest. She is driven by a powerful need to succeed, and she refuses all help. . .even from her brother's best friend, Micah Dunford. But who will stand by her when her human strength is gone?

HARVEST
Home

Harvest of Love

by Janet Lee Barton

Chapter 1

Roswell, New Mexico Territory, 1895

Liddy Evans flounced out of the bank, muttering to herself, "How dare he suggest such a thing? How could he even think I would agree to such an arrangement?"

At the end of the boardwalk, she gathered her skirts in one hand and slid a protective arm around her growing abdomen. Her mutterings continued as she stepped down onto Roswell's dusty main street and crossed over, dodging horse-drawn wagons and surreys. Safely across, she stepped up to the walk in front of Emma's Café, all the while fighting the tears that threatened.

Dear Lord, what am I to do? How can I save the farm Matthew worked so hard for?

Nothing had been easy since he'd been killed by a rattlesnake while watering his horse down by the creek.

Now this. A whole different sort of snake to contend with. There would be an answer. *There just has to be,* Liddy thought as she entered her friend's establishment.

Liddy was relieved to find the café nearly empty. Since Matthew's death, and as her delicate condition became more obvious by the day, she dreaded the pitying looks she received from the townsfolk. They meant well. She knew they did. Still, she was not one to pity herself, nor did she want the pity of others.

She sat at a table and looked around. Cal McAllister was the only other person in the café. Well, at least she'd get no pitying looks from Cal. He had suffered his own loss a couple of years back and kept pretty much to himself. As soon as Emma finished serving him, she hurried over.

She took one look at Liddy's face. "It didn't go well, did it?"

Liddy untied her bonnet and shook her head.

"You just relax while I fetch you a cup of tea and a piece of one of your pies." She hurried to the kitchen before Liddy had a chance to tell her that she didn't have much of an appetite.

Liddy leaned back in the chair to ease her aching back. Closing her eyes, she took a deep breath and prayed silently. *Dear Lord, please help me find a way to keep the farm for my child.*

Emma set a cup of tea and a large wedge of apple pie in front of her as Liddy breathed an *Amen* and opened her eyes.

"What did old Harper say to drain the color from your cheeks, Liddy?" Emma asked as she took the seat across from her.

"He won't grant an extension. If I can't make the payment by next week, he'll foreclose." Liddy shrugged and took a welcome sip of tea. "You know what chance I have of meeting that deadline?"

Emma pounded her fist on the table. "That man! He hasn't given you a moment's rest since Matthew died. I'd like to have him run out of town."

Liddy managed a small smile. "Oh, wait. You haven't heard the worst of it. He say's he's willing to pay off the loan himself, if. . ."

"If what?"

"If I'll marry him."

Emma jumped to her feet. "What? Is he crazy?"

"Well, *he* says it's the only way out."

"Liddy, you aren't thinking of—"

"No. No!" Liddy shook her head adamantly. She shuddered and closed her eyes as though attempting to shut out her pain. "I could never do that. Not even to save the farm for my child."

When she opened her eyes, she saw Calvin Mc-Allister at Emma's side. His gaze rested on Liddy, and his eyes were full of concern.

"I couldn't help but overhear part of your conversation, Mrs. Evans. Is Harper giving you problems?"

Liddy wasn't sure what to say. "I. . .he's. . ."

Emma turned to Calvin. "He's giving her problems

all right, Cal. Harper is threatening to take away Liddy's farm unless she comes up with the payment she owes by next week."

Calvin looked closer at Liddy. "Are you that much past due, Mrs. Evans?"

Liddy opened her mouth to reply that the matter was really none of his concern, but Emma didn't give her a chance.

"She's not really behind at all. She's managed to make the payments from the small amount she and Matthew had saved before he died. But that money has run out, and for the last two months she's struggled to pay, but. . ."

"Emma!" Liddy was appalled that Emma was telling Calvin McAllister her life story. He was a neighbor of sorts, but she'd never really gotten to know him. Since his wife's death, he kept pretty much to himself. About the only time she did see him was when he brought his girls to church.

She'd sent Matthew over with food when his wife passed away, and he'd been at Matthew's funeral. Other than that, she knew nothing at all about this man. Thanks to Emma, he was learning an awful lot about her.

Emma only paused for a moment. "I'm sorry, Liddy. But you aren't going to be able to keep up this pace forever. I need the pies you make and the eggs you sell me. But that heavy laundry you are taking in is going to be too hard on you before long."

Liddy barely noticed when Cal sat down at the table. Emma just kept talking. "And the gardening is going to be too much soon."

"Emma! Stop. Please." Liddy could feel the heat radiating from her face. She'd never been so embarrassed.

Finally Emma stopped her tirade and slumped back into her chair. "I'm sorry, Liddy. I just hate to see you go through this much stress so close to the baby's coming— She clamped a hand over her mouth as if to keep herself from saying anything more.

Liddy sighed in exasperation. She looked up to find Cal's warm gaze on her, a half smile on his lips. She lifted her chin a notch. "I'm sorry Emma has subjected you to my boring life, Mr. McAllister." She glared at her friend. "She's usually more discreet."

Cal chuckled and shook his head. "I don't think we know the same Emma, ma'am. She's always been one to speak her mind to me." He sat up straight. "But I regret that you've been made to feel embarrassed. I know Emma worries about you, and I'm sorry that Harper is giving you such a hard time by threatening to take your land away. His practices leave much to be desired."

"Oh, you haven't heard it all. He'll pay off the loan *if* she'll marry him! That's. . ."

"Unethical." Calvin squared his shoulders and sat straighter in the chair. "Maybe I should go have a talk with Harper."

Liddy could stand no more. "No! I couldn't ask you

to do that, Mr. McAllister. He'd only get mad and might decide to foreclose now."

"He can't do that, Mrs. Evans. Not legally. Not if your payments are up to date." His warm brown eyes met hers, and Liddy wondered why she had never noticed how good-looking he was.

She dismissed the thought with a shake of her head. "I can't let you do that. It's my problem. I thank you for your offer, though."

"Have you thought of applying for a loan at another bank?"

"Mr. McAllister, I'm a widow, with a farm that's too big for me to handle on my own. Who would give me credit?"

Cal leaned forward and propped his arms on the table. "Don't give up hope, Mrs. Evans. I think it's possible to get you out from under this stress. I'd like to help if I can."

Liddy was speechless. Calvin McAllister didn't know her. Why would he even want to try to help her? She watched as he unfolded his long legs and stood up. He dug in his pocket and pulled out some coins and laid them on the table.

"Mighty good lunch, Emma. And that was the best apple pie I believe I've ever tasted, Mrs. Evans. I'll be in touch with you soon." With that, he put his hat on and walked out the door.

Liddy looked across the table and watched a huge grin spread across Emma's face. Her friend got up and came around to hug her. "Oh, Liddy. I know Cal will come up with something! I don't know why I didn't think to ask him to help you before now."

"Emma, I can't believe it. You've been talking to him about me? Before today?"

Emma hugged her once more before reaching for their cups. "I just worry about you, Liddy. I thought he might have an idea of what to do. He's a good man, Liddy. He'll come up with something. I just know he will."

Liddy couldn't think of a reply as she watched Emma head for the kitchen. She felt dazed. It'd been a long day. She'd been up gathering eggs at dawn, after putting six pies in to bake. She'd tended her garden and picked only the best and freshest produce to bring in to Emma. After she'd delivered it all, she'd gone to the bank to ask Mr. Harper, one more time, to give her an extension on this month's payment.

She sighed deeply. What good would an extension have been anyway? Another payment would still be due next month. . .and the month after that. There was no end to them. She wanted to keep the farm for the child she was carrying, but, at the moment, there just didn't seem to be any way to do that. Unless she married Harper. A shiver slid down her spine at the very thought and she shook her head. There was no way she could or would agree to that.

Emma returned with fresh tea, and Liddy welcomed it without speaking. After several sips, she felt the anger at her friend drain away. She met Emma's smile with one of her own and shook her head.

"What am I going to do with you, Emma? You shout my life story to anyone who'll listen; make a man I barely know feel that he has to help me, then you sit here grinning like the cat who caught the canary!"

"I'm grinning because, for the first time, I feel that you may be able to keep that farm you love so much. And that Douglas Harper might be thwarted in his plans to have that farm—and you."

Liddy hid her smile behind her teacup. Emma was the best friend she'd ever known, and as exasperating as she was right this minute, she wouldn't know what to do without her. "I can assure you. Douglas Harper may well end up with my farm. But he will *never* end up with me."

Emma chuckled. "That's a relief. For it would only be over my dead body that I would let you make such a deal."

"Thank you for wanting to help me, Emma. I really do appreciate it. But unless I can figure something out, I think I may have to take you up on your generous offer to stay with you until after the baby is born."

As though on cue, the baby kicked within her. Liddy smiled and placed her hand over the movement.

"My offer still stands. You know that. But now that Cal is trying to figure something out, I don't think it will come to that."

"You seem to have gotten to know him well." Was

there something going on between Emma and Calvin? She'd thought that Emma was sweet on the new deputy in town, but. . .

"I think he just gets tired of his own cooking. And he brings the girls in a lot, too. He's really good with his girls, Liddy, but I think they need a woman's touch."

"How old are they now? I see them in church, but it's hard to tell."

"Grace is six, and Amy is nine, I believe. They're very sweet, but I think he could use some help with them."

Liddy arched her back, trying to ease the ache she frequently felt. "I'm sure it's not easy to raise children by one's self. I know the thought scares me at times."

Emma reached out and patted her hand. "You're going to do just fine. Any child of yours will be very lucky, indeed."

"I'm the lucky one. I have a part of Matthew left with me. I'll have someone to care for and love. I just wish that Matthew could have known a little one was on the way." Although she had suspected that she was in the "motherly way," she hadn't voiced her thoughts to Matthew. Her suspicions were confirmed only a few weeks after he died.

"I'm sure he does, Liddy," Emma tried to reassure her.

Liddy nodded. "Yes, I'm sure, too." She didn't need to sit here turning maudlin. She had work to do at home. "I'd better be on my way. You've got your supper crowd to get ready for. I'll get those pies and cakes to you first thing tomorrow." She eased to her feet and retied her bonnet.

She'd left her buckboard tethered around back, so Emma walked Liddy through the kitchen. The fragrant aroma of simmering stew greeted her as she entered the swinging door. Old Ben, who helped in the kitchen, looked up from his work. "How do, Mrs. Evans. Those sure were some pretty pies you brought today. They'll be gone in no time."

"Thank you Ben. I'm glad they sell well."

Emma called out after Liddy as she clambered up into the wagon. "You be careful, you hear? I think I might have to start sending Ben out after your deliveries soon. You could hurt yourself climbing in and out of that wagon."

"I'm fine, *Mother*, I promise." Liddy grinned at her friend. "I'll let you know when it gets to be too much for me."

"You'd better."

Liddy waved good-bye, and with the flick of the reins, the horse started for home. She told herself she was being silly. There was nothing Calvin McAllister could do. But, hard as she tried, she couldn't stop herself from feeling a small glimmer of hope. Maybe, just maybe, Calvin *could* find a way to help.

Chapter 2

Calvin finished loading into the back of his wagon the last of his purchases from the Jaffa-Prager Company, Roswell's large general store. The girls would be out of school soon and he would need to pick them up. He wondered if Mrs. Evans was still at the café. He still had time to tell her what his banker had said. She might, just possibly, get out from under that swine, Harper. Too bad her husband hadn't known what kind of man he was dealing with when he bought the farm.

Cal had checked out both banks in town before he'd settled on one. Douglas Harper at Harper Bank had rubbed him the wrong way the very first time they met. The men at the Bank of Roswell had always been fair in their dealings. They were good Christian men. But Douglas Harper was another breed all together. That man made his skin crawl.

He turned to cross the street just as Liddy Evans pulled her buckboard onto Main Street and headed out of town. For a moment, Cal debated about going after her, but his news would wait, and she'd looked awful tired at Emma's. There was something fragile about her. Maybe it was because she was expecting a baby and, he knew all too well, that condition could be more delicate than he'd once realized. Maybe it was that she was a widow and had no man to handle things for her.

He didn't know the reason for sure, but he did know this: Douglas Harper adding extra worry in her life right now bothered him. Bothered him a lot. Her farm wasn't far from his and he knew the land was good and fertile. What would Harper do with the property if he fore-closed? A lot of people had been looking for land in these parts lately. Maybe he just wanted to jack the price up and get richer. Or maybe he wanted it for himself. The place wasn't far out of town.

Cal pulled out his watch and looked at it. He would like to talk things over with Emma at the café, but it was nearly time for the girls to get out of school. He untied his horse, climbed up onto the wagon seat and headed for the schoolhouse, but his thoughts remained on Liddy Evans's problem.

Liddy sat by the fire brushing the shine back into her light auburn hair and thinking back over her long day. She loved working in her garden, baking for Emma's café, and taking care of her home. But she could do without the heavy laundry she took in.

She leaned back in the rocker and looked around

her home. She would hate to lose this place. Matthew had worked so hard to build it, and their life had been here in these rooms. The parlor and kitchen spread across the front with two bedrooms behind. The house wasn't a large house, but there was room to grow.

Liddy had enjoyed adding her own touches. She'd worked as fast as she could on her mother's old sewing machine to make curtains for the windows. The quilts on the bed came from her childhood home. Matthew had always taken pride in the fact that she was a good housekeeper and an even better cook.

She went to take the steaming teakettle off the fire to brew a cup of tea. She missed pouring Matthew that last cup of coffee in the evenings. They used to sit by the fire, and he would tell about his day and all the plans he had for this place.

Liddy crossed the room and eased into the rocker with her tea. She leaned her head back and sighed deeply. She missed her husband, still. She missed the companionship, the closeness of married life. The baby stirred and kicked as if to let her know that she wasn't alone. Liddy smiled and patted the spot where he'd moved.

She was sure she would always miss Matthew, but she thanked the Lord that she'd been left with his child. She would have someone to love and care for. It wouldn't be long now. Just a few more months and she'd know if she had a little boy or a girl. It didn't matter to her which, but she'd always thought of the baby as a boy. She knew she'd be happy with either and just prayed that he or she would be healthy.

Liddy took a sip of tea and put the rocker in motion. She'd provide the best she could for this child, farm or no farm. But, oh, how she wanted to be able to keep it, to let this child know how hard his father had worked to build the place up. To be able to leave the farm as an inheritance to that child one day. But that might not happen. The possibility looked less and less likely with each passing day.

Liddy admitted to a hope that Calvin McAllister could come up with a plan to help her keep the farm, but she didn't have a clue as to what that could be. Still, he was nice to even offer.

She wondered again if he and Emma were sweet on each other and wished she'd asked her friend. She'd always thought of Cal as a loner, but he and Emma certainly seemed to know each other well. She wondered how hard it was for him to be raising two daughters without a wife, and her heart filled with compassion for them.

His girls were pretty little things and were always clean and neat when they were in church. They obeyed their father and were well-behaved during service. She wondered if they took after their mother or Cal. They had his dark hair, but both had blue eyes and fair skin. Cal's complexion was darker, probably from working outside so much.

He was a very good-looking man, Liddy had to

admit. He was tall and muscular, with such warm brown eyes. And he did seem a decent man. For a moment, she felt a little envious of her friend. Then she quickly chastised herself. Emma deserved happiness. She should be happy for her.

Liddy shook her thoughts away. Well, she was sure there was no way Calvin McAllister could help. Douglas Harper wasn't going to give her an extension on paying the rest of this month's payment. He'd told her that he'd been too lenient as it was by letting her pay by the month. And there was no way to be sure about the crop this year.

The alfalfa was there. Matthew had planted it two years ago, and they'd had a really good harvest last year. It was growing nicely now, and the future of a good crop looked bright. But there was no money left to meet the payments on the loan Matthew had taken out for farm equipment and improvements. And when it was time to harvest, what then? Liddy couldn't do it herself, and there wasn't enough money left to hire help.

Well, she couldn't hire anyone, and that was all there was to it. And she was doing all she could to bring in money now. She simply didn't have enough energy or hours left in a day to do more.

The clock chimed the hour, and Liddy realized that if she was going to get up early and get the wash on the line and her baking done before the kitchen heated up, she'd better get to bed. She banked the fire and picked up the lamp. After making sure everything was locked up tight, she went to her room.

She turned down her bed, slipped under the covers, and reached for her worn Bible. God's Word brought her comfort as nothing else could. After reading several psalms, she blew out the light and said her nightly prayers. She closed her eyes, knowing that her life was in His hands, and no matter what happened with the farm, He would see her through.

The next day dawned bright and sunny. Cal hadn't slept well at all. He'd spent the better part of the night trying to figure a way to help Liddy Evans. After the restless night, he had to admit to himself that his offer to help was more than just trying to be a good neighbor.

He was attracted to her. Yet, considering her condition, he knew this fact was not something she would want to know. But he wanted to get to know her better and to find some way to help her keep her farm. He kept thinking about Mary and what if it'd been his wife who was trying to keep his place together for the girls. To think that a man like Harper would try to take advantage of a situation like that infuriated him.

Cal listened to the girls prattle as he took them to school. They were good girls, but they needed a woman's touch. Little Grace could barely remember her mother, and Amy was getting to an age where she needed a woman to teach her all kinds of things. She'd shown an interest in learning how to cook, but he was doing all he could do to get any kind of a meal on the table. And, the way he figured it, his cooking shouldn't be taught anyway. It simply wasn't that good.

The girls never complained, though. He grinned to himself. But they sure were happy when he fed them at Emma's place. He felt they needed better meals than he prepared, so he made sure they stopped at Emma's several times a week.

He'd tried to hire someone to come in and cook for him and the girls, but none of the ladies in town wanted to make the drive out to his ranch. Besides, the married ones had more than enough to do just taking care of their own families. There just wasn't a wealth of women in Roswell to begin with. Most of those that weren't married either had their own businesses, like Emma, or they simply weren't the kind of women he'd want his girls around. So, he plugged onward.

When he passed Liddy's place, the idea hit. A good idea. One that would help her out and certainly help him, too. Why hadn't he thought of it before? Cal flicked the reins and hurried the team along. He would drop the girls off and head for Emma's. He'd burnt most of the bacon this morning and given the best pieces to the girls. He could use some breakfast, and if need be, he'd wait out the rush hour so he could run his idea by Emma. But he knew already what she'd say. This idea was a good one. He just knew it was.

Liddy pulled up to the back of Emma's Café. Three cakes and three more apple pies sat covered with cloth

25

on the floor of the wagon. Ben rushed out to help her carry them in.

"Just in time, Mrs. Evans. A few minutes ago, Miss Emma served the last piece of pie we had in the kitchen. She told me to ask if you would have time for coffee this morning."

Liddy set the last pie on the worktable in the kitchen and smiled at the old man. "I'll make time, Ben. She's out front?"

"Yes, ma'am, she sure is."

Liddy headed through the swinging door into the dining room. She knew Emma always had a crowd for breakfast, but by this time of day, the café would be clearing out, and only those who had time to savor a second cup of coffee would be left.

Emma looked up from the cash box and grinned at her. "I'm so glad you are here. Cal's been waiting for you."

Surprised, Liddy looked around the room and found him at a table by the front window, looking into his coffee cup as if he were a million miles away.

"Cal? You mean, Mr. McAllister?" She wasn't thrilled when her heartbeat sped up.

Emma grabbed her by the hand and practically dragged her across the room. "One and the same. He wants to talk to you."

Was it possible? Had he come up with an idea? Liddy was afraid to hope, but that was exactly what she did as Cal looked up at her and immediately got to his feet.

"Mrs. Evans. I was hoping to have a chance to talk to you. Would you join me for breakfast or a cup of coffee?"

Emma gave her a little shove and she found herself sitting in the chair across from Calvin McAllister. "I. . . ah. . .I'll take a cup of tea, thank you."

Emma immediately scurried away and was back in a flash with a clean cup and a fresh pot of tea. She filled Liddy's cup and then said, "If you'll both excuse me, I have things to do in the back."

Some friend, Liddy thought, as Emma disappeared into the kitchen. *She spills my life history to the man and then won't stick around to see what he has to say.*

Cal cleared his throat and brought her attention back to him. "Mrs. Evans, I think I may have come up with a plan to help you and myself in the process. I. . . uh. . .I have a proposition I'd like to put to you."

Liddy felt color flooding her face. Another one? What was wrong with the men in this town? She was a widow, not a year yet, not to mention, *she was with child.* She started to stand.

Cal got to his feet once more and held out his hand. "Oh, no, Mrs. Evans. Not like that. What I meant to say was. . .a *business* proposition. Nothing like Harper. Please. Stay and hear me out."

Chapter 3

L iddy looked into Calvin's eyes and saw the earn-
estness in his expression. Maybe she had jumped
to the wrong conclusion. She hoped so. She
settled back in the chair.

"All right, Mr. McAllister. I'll hear you out."

He sat back down and let out a sigh. "I'm sorry. I
don't always think before I speak." Liddy's heart did a
little flip at his smile. He looked like a little boy trying
to talk his way out of a jam.

"First, I talked to my banker. He'd like to help, but
you were right. His board of directors wouldn't consider
you a good risk."

Liddy felt her heart drop. She knew that, but still
she'd allowed herself to hope. She nodded. "I expected
as much, Mr. McAllister. All the same, I thank you for
trying."

"He did have another idea, though. He suggested
that you lease part or all of the land."

Liddy's eyebrows drew together. "Lease it?"

Cal leaned back in his chair and grinned at her. "That's where you let someone else farm your land. They pay you for using it, usually after harvest, from the profits off the crops."

Liddy spread her hands out and shook her head. "That's something I wish I'd known earlier, Mr. McAllister. It won't help me now. I don't have time to wait for harvest."

Cal leaned forward and pushed his plate out of the way, propping his forearms on the table. "I realize that, but what if someone paid you half up front and the balance at harvest?"

Liddy leaned back in her chair and chuckled. "That would be wonderful, but I don't think that's likely to happen."

"If you'll agree to let me lease your land, it will."

"You? But, well, I—"

"I had a really good crop last year, and I've wanted to expand for some time now. I'd appreciate it if you would lease to me, Mrs. Evans. I'd give you a fair price."

Liddy could only gape at the figure he gave her. She wasn't sure she could believe her ears. This was the way out. With the advance on the lease, she could pay ahead until harvest, and with the final payment from Mr. McAllister, she would be able to pay the balance for the year.

"Mr. McAllister, I don't know what to say. Of course I accept your offer. I. . .thank you."

Cal rubbed the back of his neck and smiled at her.

"I'm glad. I do have another favor to ask you."

A favor to ask her? After what he was offering to do for her? "Of course; what can I do for you?"

"You know I have two daughters? Grace is the little one and Amy is my oldest."

"They are very pretty little girls, Mr. McAllister." Liddy wondered where he was leading with this.

"Well, I'm not a very good cook. And I don't know how to teach them how. Wouldn't want to teach them to cook like I do, anyway. I tried to get a housekeeper. Even ran a few advertisements in the paper, but got no answer."

Did he want her as a housekeeper? He wasn't suggesting anything more, was he? After Douglas Harper's proposition, she was more than a little apprehensive.

"You want me to be your housekeeper?"

"No. No! I just want you to teach Amy a little about cooking and both of them how to help me keep house. I don't expect her to cook five-course meals or anything like that. Just maybe learn a few things that would help me out. And I don't expect them to do heavy cleaning, just maybe how to dust and pick up?"

Liddy couldn't contain the burst of relieved laughter that escaped. "Oh, that's it? That's all you want me to do?"

"Seems like quite a lot to me. I don't have the first idea how to go about teaching them the things their mother would have been teaching them."

Liddy's heart went out to the man. She wasn't going to have any idea how to teach her child, if it were a boy, all the manly things he needed to know.

"I'll be glad to take your girls under my wing, Mr. McAllister. It will be a pleasure."

"I'll pay you extra—"

"No, sir, you will not."

"Yes, ma'am, I will. With teaching the girls those things, you won't be having time to take in that laundry anymore. And I won't take charity from you any more than you would take it from me."

"But—"

"No arguments." Cal shook his head. "I'll not ask you to take on more work and give up income to do that, without paying you." He held out his right hand. "Do we have a deal, Mrs. Evans?"

Did they have a deal? Did he think she was crazy? Or was he crazy? Either way, there was only one answer as far as Liddy was concerned. "We have a deal, Mr. McAllister."

Her hand was swallowed by his larger, work-callused grip in a shake that sent little splinters of electricity up her arm. The jolt was an unwelcome surprise. Liddy quickly pulled her hand back.

"When, ah, when do you want me to start with the girls? After school today?"

Cal shook his head. "Not today. You need time to let the people you've been doing wash for know that you'll no longer be available. Why don't we start Monday? That will give you several days to get things in order and get some rest."

Dear Lord, thank You. I don't know why You sent this man into my life, but I thank You for this blessing.

"That will be fine, Mr. McAllister. I'll be looking forward to meeting your daughters." Liddy took a sip of tea, not sure what to say next. How did you say thank you to someone for saving your life?

"I think this is going to work out well, Mrs. Evans. I'll have my lawyer draw up the lease agreement, unless you'd prefer to have yours—"

"No, that's fine. I trust you, Mr. McAllister."

"I'll have a bank draft drawn up and bring it to you. Will you be in town for a while? If not, I can drop the draft by your place."

"I have some supplies to pick up. I'll wait, if you don't mind. Then I can take the payment to my bank and get that debt off my mind."

Cal grinned at her. "And I'll even accompany you, if you'd like. I wouldn't mind getting a look at Harper's face when you make that payment."

Relief replaced her dread of facing Douglas Harper by herself. "Thank you. I think I'll take you up on that offer. I don't like. . ." How could she say she didn't like the way the man leered at her? There was something about Harper that made her heart grow cold each time she was in his presence. She'd be glad for the company.

"I don't like him much myself. I'll find you around town and we'll go over together." Cal stood up and put coins down for his bill. He put his hat on and lowered the brim at Liddy.

"Ma'am, I'll see you a little later." With that, he turned and walked out the door.

Liddy willed her heartbeat to slow as she looked around for Emma, wanting to share the news with her.

Emma appeared at her elbow almost immediately. She poured them both a fresh cup of tea and set between them a plate of sweet rolls from the batch that Liddy had baked and delivered yesterday.

"Oh, Emma." Liddy felt dazed. She still couldn't believe what was happening. She shook her head, and then threw it back, her laughter filling the dining room.

"You said yes! Oh, Liddy, I'm so glad. This is the answer to your problems." Emma reached out and clasped Liddy's hands with her own. "I told you Cal would find a way."

"I can't believe it, Emma. Why didn't I think of leasing my land?"

"Well, there's not a lot of leasing done around here. I did hear that Douglas Harper has been buying up all the land he can. I guess some people would rather sell than lease, but for you it seems to be an answer to a prayer!"

"Oh, Emma, it is. Do you realize that I can pay several months ahead with the bank payments, and with the earnings from the harvest, I might be able to pay up until next year?"

Emma nodded at her. "And, what's even better, Douglas Harper will have to leave you alone."

"Praise the Lord! Oh, Emma, He does know our

needs and finds the best ways to fill them. You're a very lucky woman, you know."

"Me? I've got a lot of blessings, to be sure, but I'd think you are the lucky one today, Liddy. To have Calvin McAllister taking up your cause. . ."

"Emma, are you upset that he's helping me?"

"Upset? Liddy, I'm delighted! You should know that."

"It won't cause problems between the two of you, to have his girls at my house, and him letting them off and picking them up?"

"Liddy, the day's events must have scrambled your mind." Emma looked confused for a moment, then burst into laughter. "So that's it? You thought Cal and I were interested in each other?"

Liddy grinned and nodded her head.

Emma wiped tears from her eyes and shook her head. "Oh, Liddy, you are such a goose. Cal is a wonderful man, but, no, we are *not* interested in each other that way. He's just become a good friend." She leaned closer to Liddy and whispered, "Besides, I have my sights set on that new deputy in town."

The relief Liddy felt was more than it should be, considering her current condition. Yet, knowing that fact didn't keep it from washing over her, just the same. "Well, when are you going to let the deputy in on how you feel?"

Emma snorted delicately. "Not until I'm certain the feeling is mutual. He's about as dense as a horse, that's for sure."

Liddy laughed again and, as she did, she realized that she hadn't done much laughing in a long time. It felt really good to join her friend in shared fun.

She gathered her purse and stood up, brushing crumbs from her dress. "I'd better get my shopping done. Cal—Mr. McAllister—is going to bring me a draft to take to the bank before I leave town. He's even going to go with me when I make the payment."

Emma stood too and began to clear the table. "Oh, wouldn't I love to be a mouse in the room. Douglas Harper isn't going to be very happy today."

"I know. But I surely am!" Liddy grinned at her. She waved to Emma and, though she felt like twirling out the door, she forced herself to step sedately out onto the boardwalk.

Chapter 4

Liddy took a deep breath and pondered how much brighter the day had become. The sky was a cloudless blue, the sun warm. Her heart was singing for the first time since Matthew's death. She would be able to keep the farm he'd worked so hard to start, and she would be able to take care of the child that grew in her womb. God was so good. Over and over again, she silently gave thanks as she made her way to Jaffa-Prager Company.

Letting herself relax, she wandered across the store selecting her purchases, and was only half finished when Cal found her.

"Are you ready to take a load off your mind, Mrs. Evans?" He handed her the bank draft.

Liddy looked at the amount and her spurt of laughter brought curious looks from the other shoppers. "I'm ready, Mr. McAllister." She took the arm he offered and told the storekeeper that she'd be back shortly to finish her shopping.

The walk to the bank was short, but not too short for Liddy to feel protected in a way she hadn't in months. She missed the courtesies of having a man to guide her across the rough and dusty streets, to open a door for her.

They entered the bank, and it took a moment for Liddy's eyes to adjust from the bright outdoors to the dimness of the interior. She walked up to the teller.

"I'd like to deposit this into my account, please." She handed him the slip of paper. "And then I'd like to write a draft out to the bank for the balance of my note payment this month and also make next month's payment."

The teller looked at her and shot a nervous glance at Cal, before looking toward the back of the building. "Yes, ma'am. I'll. . .I'll get the amount of that payment and be right with you." He quickly hightailed it from behind the teller's cage to the door of Harper's office.

He'd barely entered before he reemerged, Harper shoving him out of the way as he headed toward Liddy and Cal.

"What's this, Liddy? You've come to pay your note? After our talk yesterday, I thought—"

"You thought there was no way I would be able to meet my obligations, Mr. Harper. But here I am."

"Yes, well, why don't we talk about it? If you'll just step into my office. . ." His pudgy hand motioned to the room he'd just left.

Liddy shook her head and smiled. "There's no need to talk. I have the payment right here. If your clerk will be so kind as to deposit this draft into my account and let me write my own out to the bank, I'll be on my way."

"But, Liddy, I'd be interested to know how you came into this money. Have you sold your land?"

Calvin stepped up. "No, Harper, she hasn't sold out. She's agreed to lease her land to me."

"Lease? To you?"

"That's right."

"I didn't know that you were wanting to expand, McAllister."

Cal cocked an eyebrow. "No reason I can see why you should know."

"Yes, well. . ." Harper looked away and glared at the teller. "Deposit Liddy's draft and let her write her own to the bank, Nelson."

Cal smiled at the clerk. "And please make sure *Mrs. Evans* gets a receipt for her payments."

Harper blustered. "Yes. . .well. Nelson, see to it." He turned on his heel and scurried back to his office.

Cal watched as the clerk finished the transaction and Liddy had the receipt firmly in hand. He crooked his arm and smiled down at Liddy. "I'll see you back to the general store, Mrs. Evans."

Once out into the bright sunshine again, Liddy turned to Cal and released a huge sigh of relief. "Mr. McAllister, again, I thank you. I believe I'll sleep well tonight."

Cal inclined his head. "I hope you do. If you're

feeling up to it, we can walk over to my lawyer's office. He should have the contract ready by now."

Suddenly, the realization struck Liddy that he'd put his trust in her by giving her the draft before they'd even signed the contract. She wanted to honor that trust as soon as possible. "Let's go get those papers signed."

The attorney's office was light and airy compared to that of the bank. Cal's lawyer saw them both into his office and went over the simple contract. Liddy had no reason to feel apprehensive about anything. The agreement was for a year at a time, with options for her to agree or not, to each renewal.

After being asked if she had any questions, she signed over the right to farm her husband's land to another man. But she didn't feel the least bit bad. It was what Matthew would have wanted her to do, to keep the land for their child.

The lawyer shook their hands, and Cal took her elbow to lead her outdoors once more. He saw her back to the general store as promised, then turned to her. "Thank you for trusting me with your land, Mrs. Evans. I promise to take good care of it."

Liddy shielded her eyes from the lowering sun. "I know you will, Mr. McAllister." She smiled at him. "And I promise to take good care of your girls."

"Speaking of whom, I'd best be picking them up from school. I know they're going to be excited about having you teach them." He tipped his hat and smiled down at her. "I'll be talking to you, ma'am."

Liddy watched him walk toward the schoolhouse before she turned into the store. The realization that she no longer had to pinch her pennies quite so hard made her feel quivery on the inside. She still couldn't quite take it all in. She might actually buy a length of material to make another dress. She'd let out what she had as far as they would go. And she still had weeks to go before the baby was due.

However, as she looked at the colorful bolts of material, she realized how exhausted she was from the day's events. Or was it just the lifting of the worry that made her feel ready to drop? No matter. She just wanted to get home, to think about all that had happened, and to enjoy the knowledge that she wouldn't have to move.

She hurriedly gathered up the rest of her purchases, adding a tin of her favorite tea to the pile. The boxes were totaled, loaded into her buckboard, and she was on her way home.

Liddy passed the school on her way out of town and saw Cal helping his daughters into his wagon. They were both talking to him at once, and she could tell by the smile on his face that he was enjoying their excitement.

In her haste to get back home, she forgot to tell the hotel that she wouldn't be doing the wash for them anymore. *Oh, well,* she thought, *the matter can wait.* She had to deliver fresh linens to them tomorrow. She grinned to herself. They would simply have to find someone else to wash their dirty laundry.

At home, she carefully unloaded her purchases. She

must ask Mr. Carmack to make the packages lighter for a while. Her back was aching by the time she finished, but she knew if she sat down, she'd never get her afternoon chores finished.

After putting the kettle on for tea, she changed into her everyday dress and a fresh apron. She made a cup of tea and let herself pause to look out the front door at the land that she would now be sharing with Calvin McAllister. Things might not be working out the way she'd thought they should, but they were working out.

She hoped his daughters would be open to learning what she could teach them, and she prayed that the Lord would show her how to be sensitive to their feelings. They might possibly resent being taught by someone who wasn't their mother. Her heart filled with compassion for them. After the last few days, she was sure Calvin was a good and loving father to them, but still, he could only do so much.

Liddy sighed as the thought reminded her that she'd have the same problem soon. To try and be both mother and father to a child was a daunting thought. She must trust the Lord to lead her. She turned from the doorway and went to get her laundry basket. The sheets she'd washed that morning would be dry by now. She still had much work to do before she could relax.

❦

Calvin pointed out Liddy's farm as he drove the girls home.

"That's it, Papa? That's where we're going to learn

to cook and clean?" Amy asked, her voice rising with excitement.

"That's it, darlin', and I think you are going to really like Mrs. Evans. She's a nice lady."

Grace craned her neck as they drove by. "Is that her out at the clothesline, Papa?"

Cal turned his head and saw Liddy at the clothesline, struggling with a sheet. He turned the wagon around and pulled into her yard. "Stay here, girls."

His long stride took him quickly to Liddy's side, and he pushed her hands away from the sheet. "Didn't you let these people know you won't be working for them any longer?" he asked, his tone rougher than he intended.

"Mr. McAllister, what are you doing here? No. I didn't let them know. I was tired and figured to tell them tomorrow when I take this laundry in to the hotel." Liddy stood aside as he quickly added the sheet to the pile already in the basket.

He picked it up easily and headed for the house. "Where do you want these?"

Liddy hurried ahead of him. "On the kitchen table will be fine. Thank you."

"You shouldn't be doing this kind of work." Cal noticed her shortness of breath as she hurried beside him, the faint shadows beneath her eyes. She was exhausted.

He couldn't help but notice how neat and clean her home was. Next to his, it would have been impossible not to make the comparison. She motioned to the table, and he set the basket down. "You will tell them tomorrow? That you won't be taking in their wash anymore?"

Liddy smiled at him, but he didn't miss the fact that she'd placed a hand at the base of her back. Obviously, her back was bothering her. "I'll tell them, Mr. McAllister. And I have you to thank that I won't be needing to do it anymore."

Cal nodded. He just wished he'd been able to help sooner. "Well, I guess I'd best be getting the girls home."

"They're outside? May I meet them?"

"Of course. They were very excited to learn that you will be teaching them to cook and clean." He went to the door and motioned for her to go in front of him.

The girls were patiently waiting, but he could see them smiling as he and Liddy moved closer to the wagon.

"Mrs. Evans, I'd like you to meet my daughters. The little one is Grace, and the older one is Amy." A sense of pride swept over him as his girls both smiled at Liddy.

"Pleased to meet you, ma'am," Amy said. Grace nodded her head in agreement.

"It's very nice to meet you both. I'm looking forward to our time together."

"Are we really going to learn to cook, Mrs. Evans?" Amy asked.

"You certainly are."

Amy's smile lit up her face. "Oh, I'm so glad. Will

we learn to cook something besides bacon and beans?"

Liddy chuckled and slid a glance toward Cal.

He joined the laugher. "Now you know what my girls live on, mostly."

"I promise I'll teach you to cook more than bacon and beans. Although, those are things you'll need to learn, too. But we won't start with them."

Grace clapped her hands together. "Could we learn to make desserts? We only have them when we eat at Miss Emma's. Those sure are good pies at Miss Emma's."

"Well, you are in luck, Grace," Cal said. "Know who makes those pies?"

Grace shook her head.

Cal reached out and tousled her hair. "Mrs. Evans makes them."

Grace's eyes grew round with delight as she looked at Liddy. "You do? Really?"

"Will we learn to make pies, too, Mrs. Evans?" Amy fairly bounced in the seat.

"I promise to teach you to make pies."

Both girls clapped their hands. "Oh, I can't wait to get started, Mrs. Evans," Amy said.

Liddy smiled at both girls. "I'm looking forward to it myself."

"Well, I guess we'd better be on our way." Cal looked down at Liddy. He was pleased that she and the girls had obviously taken a liking to each other. Liddy Evans was going to be good for them.

"I'll look forward to Monday, Grace and Amy,"

Liddy said. "But I'll see you in church on Sunday, too."

Cal turned before he climbed into the wagon. "You try to get a little rest before then, you hear?"

He watched as a faint pink color crept up Liddy's cheeks. She waved a good-bye to them all as she nodded and replied, "I'll surely try, Mr. McAllister."

"Papa, she's really nice, isn't she?" Amy asked when their wagon turned onto the road.

"She really is, Amy."

"Papa, is she going to have a baby?"

Cal nodded. "Yes, she is. I want you girls to be very good for her and mind what she says, you hear?"

Grace leaned her head against him. "We will, Papa."

Amy met his eyes and smiled. "We will," she assured him. "Where's her husband, Papa?"

"She's a widow, honey."

"Oh. She must be very lonesome. But she will feel better when the baby gets here."

Cal hadn't let himself think about that. Liddy probably was very lonesome. He had his girls, yet still, he felt lonesome at times. Now he looked over at their shining heads and wondered what he would do without them. He smiled at Amy, wanting to reassure her. "You're right. She'll feel much better when the baby gets here, honey. I'm sure she will."

He knew from experience, this was true. But, while children could carve out their very own spot in one's heart, they couldn't fill that soul-deep void that came with the loss of a mate. Alone in her home, with her child not yet here, Cal was sure that Liddy Evans felt that emptiness very acutely. He hoped having his girls around would help.

Chapter 5

Liddy poured herself a cup of tea and carried it to the rocker. She sat down with a sigh of relief. Her work was done for the day. The sheets were ironed and folded and put neatly into the baskets. No longer would she have to do mountains of laundry for other people. She leaned her head back and smiled.

Calvin McAllister's daughters were delightful, and she found herself really looking forward to teaching them. He'd done a good job on his own. They were polite and well behaved. Seeing the job he'd done, she felt that there was hope for her to raise her own child alone.

He was a good man. It had felt good to have him carry in the basket of sheets. It'd been so long since she'd had anyone around to do the simplest things for her. She still couldn't quite take in the fact that she didn't have to worry about Douglas Harper foreclosing on her farm.

Dear Lord, I thank You for bringing this man into my life. For letting there be a way for me to keep the farm.

You've always seen to my needs, and I'm sorry I worried so.

The Scriptures were right. One shouldn't worry about tomorrow; it would take care of itself. The Lord would see to tomorrow.

Liddy sipped her tea and thought about the next week, and how nice it would be to have the girls around. She would try to teach them simple, basic cooking at first. And of course, desserts. Pies had always been her favorite thing to prepare. She didn't find them difficult, as some women did. She hoped she could teach the girls in a way that would make it easy for them.

A huge yawn escaped her and she hurriedly finished her tea. It was time for bed. Tomorrow she would plan some more. She wished she knew what foods Mr. McAllister particularly liked. After all he was doing for her, she'd like to make sure the girls learned to make some of his favorite dishes.

Cal checked on his daughters and found them fast asleep. They had kicked off their covers, so he pulled the blankets back over them again, then he bent to kiss each girl gently on the forehead. He smiled to himself as he made his way back downstairs. They hadn't complained about the beans and bacon they'd eaten for supper, but they had said how it wouldn't be long until they would be cooking for him.

He was glad they were excited about learning from Liddy. He just hoped the girls wouldn't prove too much for her. She did look tired this evening. Still, her eyes had been shining. He was glad he'd helped to put the shine in them. He would have hoped that someone would have helped Mary out, had she been the one left alone.

Cal poured the last cup of coffee and settled down in front of the fire. He wondered if Liddy had been able to sit a spell before going to bed. He'd noticed she had a rocker pulled close to the fireplace, too. Was she sitting there now?

She was a pretty woman, glowing because of the child she carried. He wondered if she would have a girl or a boy. Would she name it after her husband if it were a boy? Matthew had been a good man, a hard worker. They hadn't known each other real well, but they'd exchanged pleasantries when they'd met at the general store or on the street. Cal hadn't really ever talked to Liddy until recently. But, then again, why would he? She was a married woman.

Now she was a widow. Expecting a child. He'd do well to remember that fact. He found it too easy to get lost in her green eyes. Not liking or wanting to admit the direction his thoughts were taking him, Cal gulped down his coffee and turned in for the night.

⁂

Sunday dawned bright and beautiful. After putting several pies in the oven to bake, Liddy hurried through her morning chores. She dressed in one of only two dresses that she could still fit into and promised herself that she would shop for material the next day. She took special care with her hair, pulling the locks up into a soft knot.

Liddy loved Sundays. She only did the chores that had to be done, and she looked forward to going to church. She loved the fellowship, the lesson, and the singing. Covering the pies with clean cloths, she placed them under the seat of the wagon, which she'd hitched earlier. Carefully climbing up onto the seat, she headed for town.

Greeted by several members as she entered the church, she was smiling as she took her seat beside Emma.

"You're coming home with me for dinner, aren't you?" Emma asked.

Liddy nodded. "I'm looking forward to it." They'd made plans when Liddy had come into town with the laundry on Friday. She hadn't relaxed fully until she'd told the hotel manager that she wouldn't be doing the laundry anymore. He hadn't been too happy, but he'd paid her and wished her well.

Liddy looked across the aisle as Calvin and his daughters arrived. The girls settled down quickly but caught Liddy's eye and smiled excitedly. Grace tugged at her father's arm, and he looked over at Liddy, nodded, and smiled.

She told herself that the racing of her heart was just excitement in looking forward to the next day, and turned her attention to the service. As always, the singing uplifted her. The lesson was a good one, on trusting the Lord in all things.

Liddy felt peace in her soul. She knew how well the Lord took care of her, and she said a silent prayer of thanksgiving. The service was over all too soon and Liddy and Emma stood to leave.

Calvin and his daughters stepped into the aisle at the same time. "Morning, ladies. I hope you have a nice day."

Amy smiled up at them. "Hello, Miss Emma and Mrs. Evans."

"Good morning, Amy and Grace. Thank you, Mr. McAllister. I'm sure we will. I'm having dinner with Emma. But first, I have something for the girls, if you'd be so kind as to follow me out to my wagon?"

"For the girls? Mrs. Evans, you don't have to—"

"I know that, Mr. McAllister," Liddy said as they moved to the back of the church, the girls and Emma behind them. "It's not that much. Just something I wanted to do."

Calvin's daughters and Emma were whispering behind them, and Liddy turned just as Emma gave them both a wink.

"Cal, why don't you bring the girls over to the café for dinner, too? My treat today."

"You're closed on Sundays, Emma. You deserve a break."

"Having friends over is a break for me. Please come join us."

Cal looked at Liddy, and she smiled at him. It would

give her a chance to know the girls better before tomorrow. "Please do. We'd love to have the girls and you join us." They drew alongside her wagon and Liddy stopped beside it.

"I made a pie for you and the girls, and one to take to Emma's. But we can all have ours for dessert, and you can take the other home."

Amy and Grace clapped their hands. "Oh, thank you, Mrs. Evans! What kind is it?"

The adults all chuckled at their enthusiasm. "It's apple," Liddy said. "Do you like that kind?"

"It's my favorite," Grace said.

"Mine too," Amy added.

"Well, good. And we can all enjoy it together." She handed one pie to Amy and one to Grace. "You be careful with them. We wouldn't want to eat dusty apple pie."

Both girls giggled, and each carried a pie as carefully as if they were glass baubles.

"That was very nice of you, Mrs. Evans."

"It was the least I could do, Mr. McAllister."

"Oh, for goodness sake." Emma stopped in the middle of the street and put her hands on her hips. "When are you two going to stop this Mrs. Evans, Mr. McAllister business? Takes you forever to get out what you are going to say. Liddy, this is Cal. Cal, Liddy."

Cal grinned at Liddy. "Hello, Liddy. I am pleased to make your acquaintance."

She smiled back. "Hello, Mr.—Cal."

Emma continued on her way. "Well, that's better. If

you are going to be seeing each other nearly every day, it will make conversation much easier."

Liddy and Cal chuckled as they followed Emma and the girls into her restaurant.

Emma left them with orders to set the table while she went to check on the roast she'd put on earlier.

Liddy took off her hat and found an apron for her and the girls. She showed them how to set the table with the fork on the left and the knife and spoon on the right.

Cal found a two-day-old copy of the *Roswell Register*, one of the town's two newspapers, to keep him occupied while Liddy and the girls helped Emma finish preparing the meal and carry the food to the table.

Once they were all seated, Cal said the blessing, and Emma asked him to serve the meat as they started the meal.

Liddy couldn't remember the last time she had enjoyed a dinner quite so much. Grace and Amy's manners were wonderful, and she approved that Cal hadn't raised them to be timid as they joined in the conversation, regaling the adults with stories from school.

The afternoon passed far too quickly, and soon Cal and his girls were ready to take their leave. He'd left to bring Liddy's wagon from the church to the café, while she and the girls helped Emma with the clean up.

Liddy made sure they took the rest of the pie with them, and Cal and the girls thanked her profusely.

She and Emma took tea out to the back porch as

they wound down. "Emma, that was awfully nice of you to invite Cal and his family to join us. I enjoyed it immensely."

Emma gave her a grin. "I could tell. I did too. Cal has done a good job with the girls. They're a pleasure to be around."

Liddy took a sip of tea and nodded. "I'm really looking forward to teaching them how to cook and clean. They seem to be excited about it, too."

Emma chuckled. "I think they are a little tired of Cal's cooking."

"You know, Emma, I still can't believe that I don't have to worry about the farm being taken away. The Lord has answered my prayers a hundredfold."

Emma patted her shoulder. "I'm glad. I knew He'd see to it that you kept the farm. I'm just glad Cal was the one the Lord sent to help you. I trust him. He's an honorable man."

"Yes, he is." Liddy stretched, and then chuckled when the baby did a flip. "And it's such a relief that I can bring my child into the world and not worry if I'll be able to provide for him." She rubbed a hand over the child she carried.

"He or she is going to be a lucky little one to have you for a mother, Liddy."

"As would a child of yours, Emma. And that reminds me, how are things going with you and Deputy Johnson?"

Emma sighed. "They aren't. I asked him to dinner

today, too, but he declined, saying there was no one to watch the jail if he were to come here. The sheriff is out of town."

"You could always take him a plate, Emma. I'm sure he would appreciate such an act of kindness."

"Do you really think I should? That's rather bold, isn't it?"

Liddy shook her head. "Think of it as an act of Christian kindness. You don't have to tarry. Just take the plate to him and leave." She grinned at Emma. "Let him taste your cooking and think about what a nice gesture that was and what a great cook you are."

"I could do that."

"Of course you can. And he'll have to return the plate and thank you." Liddy grinned at her friend.

Emma giggled. "Oh, Liddy, you do have the best ideas!"

Before taking her leave, Liddy accompanied Emma to the kitchen and helped her put together a plate to take to the deputy.

Outside, Liddy climbed into her wagon and looked down at Emma. "You be sure and let me know how it goes, you hear?"

Emma held the plate in her hand, ready to take it to the sheriff's office. "You can be certain I will. Let's just hope some other eligible female hasn't had the same idea."

"Well, you aren't going to know that until you take it to him. Go on, take that man some food." Liddy waved at her friend and turned her horse toward home.

It had been a wonderful day. She was really looking forward to the next afternoon. A tiny part of her acknowledged that she was looking forward to seeing not only the girls, but their father as well. She pushed the thought aside. She had no business thinking that way.

Yet, even after she changed her clothes and went about her evening chores, her thoughts kept returning to the tall, handsome farmer. She felt rather disloyal even thinking of him. She had lost her Matthew only seven months ago. Surely that wasn't long enough for her to be thinking about another man in this way.

Dear Lord, please forgive me. I know I'm lonely, but it's not time to think of someone else, is it?

She struggled to put Calvin McAllister out of her mind and began by planning what cooking project she would first attempt with the girls. A good stew might be nice. And biscuits. Those should be easy enough. The art of baking bread would come later.

Liddy busied herself until bedtime and, as she settled down with her Bible once more, she thanked the Lord again for taking such good care of her. But as she closed her eyes for sleep, she couldn't keep her heart from beating a little faster at the thought of seeing Calvin McAllister the next day.

Chapter 6

Liddy watched the clock the next afternoon as she waited for Cal to bring the girls out to her. Early that morning, she had baked several cakes and pies and delivered them to Emma. After that, she'd shopped for the material she'd promised herself. Today had been a good day, and a much easier one without the laundry to do for the hotel.

She heard the sound of horse hooves outside and went to the door with a smile on her face.

Cal helped the girls down from the wagon and turned to Liddy. "Don't let them tire you, all right? They don't need to learn everything at once."

Liddy shielded her eyes against the sun. "We'll be fine. How long do we have?"

"I'll pick them up at sunset, if that's all right with you?"

"That will be fine. We'll have plenty of time that way."

Cal tipped his hat to her. "I'll see you then. Girls, mind your manners now."

"We will, Papa," they chimed together.

Liddy led them inside and found a couple of aprons for them to put on. "How does a menu of stew and biscuits sound to you, girls?"

"Mmm, sounds wonderful to me," Amy answered.

"Me, too," Grace said. "It'll sure beat those old beans we eat all the time."

Liddy chuckled and set the girls to work. Grace scrubbed the vegetables and Liddy showed Amy how to cut them in uniform pieces. Then, Liddy showed them how to cut up a chunk of pork by doing it herself.

She cautioned them about the use of the cookstove, and how they had to be really careful with the fire.

Amy looked over her shoulder as she browned the meat and then she pulled up a stool for Grace so that she could watch as they added the chopped vegetables to the pot. Liddy added some water last, and they watched and waited until it came to a boil. Then she covered the pan and slid it into the oven.

"Oh, the stew already smells so good," Grace said, as she helped with cleaning up the table so they could use it once more to learn how to make biscuits.

"It really does." Amy agreed. "Won't Papa be happy to smell that when he comes to get us?"

Liddy smiled, listening to their chatter as she got out the ingredients for the biscuits. "We don't need to start these just yet. Let's see. We have the stew and there will be biscuits. You have the pie for dessert."

At their downcast faces and the shaking of their heads, Liddy chuckled. "You finished the pie already?"

Amy nodded. "It was just so good. Papa let us have some after supper last night."

Grace shook her head up and down. "And we had the rest for breakfast and our lunch. Papa put a piece for each of us in our lunch pails. He didn't even save a piece for himself."

Liddy smiled. "Well, maybe we can think of something else for dessert." Both girls smiled and nodded.

"We'll make a quick peach cobbler. That will be easy, and we can use some of the biscuit dough for that."

She led the girls down into the cellar and picked a jar of peaches she'd put up the year before. She pointed out where things were located, in case she sent either of them down for something. She was proud of her cellar. She'd canned everything she could get her hands on last year and would do the same in the coming months. She wanted to be sure that she'd have enough to take her through the winter so she wouldn't have to spend quite so much at Jaffa-Prager Company. Or, if she were snowed in, she wouldn't have to make the trip with a new baby.

The sun was lowering by the time they climbed the stairs once more. She showed them how to check the stew and prick the meat to see if it was done. Then they started the biscuits.

She let Amy cut the lard into the flour, baking powder, and salt, and showed Grace how to make a well and add the milk. Liddy cautioned them not to overwork the dough as she kneaded it lightly and turned it out onto a floured board. She let Grace roll out the dough and Amy cut out the rounds.

They both helped to put them in the baking pan. Liddy slid the stew out of the oven and put it to the back of the stovetop. The biscuits were slid into the oven. She talked the girls through opening the jar of peaches, adding a little sugar, cinnamon, and flour to thicken the juice, then mixing it well in a baking dish. Next, they rolled out the biscuit dough and cut it into strips to place over the peaches. The pan was added to the oven and they started cleaning up.

The smells wafting around them made Grace's stomach start to growl, and they were all laughing when Cal knocked on the door.

"Oh, I'm sorry, Mr.—Cal. Time got away from us. This will all be ready in just a few minutes. Let me dip up some stew for my supper, and you can go ahead and load it into your wagon."

"Papa, we made stew and biscuits and a cobbler from the leftover biscuit dough and, oh, I know it's going to be so good," Grace rambled.

"From the way my stomach is growling at those smells, I can tell it's going to be great," Cal said as he tweaked Grace's nose.

He looked at Liddy as she dipped up a bowl of the stew for her own supper. "They did all right?"

Liddy smiled. "Why, they did more than all right. They are naturals. They're going to learn very quickly."

Both Amy and Grace beamed at her compliment.

Liddy handed Amy a potholder. "Amy, would you like to check the biscuits and the cobbler and tell me what color they are?"

Anxious to show off some of her newly learned skill for her father, Amy took the pot holder and eased the oven door open. "They're a beautiful golden brown, Mrs. Evans."

"Then it's time to take them out. Do you need some help?"

Amy shook her head and carefully lifted the pan of biscuits out of the oven. She placed them on the work-table and went back for the cobbler.

Cal sniffed appreciatively. "Oh, peach cobbler. That's one of my favorites. You've outdone yourselves, ladies."

Liddy took a biscuit for her meal and used clean dishtowels to cover the rest and the cobbler. "There you go. A meal fit for a king. I hope you all enjoy it." She smiled as she handed a pot holder over to Cal and then handed him the pot of stew. "Let's get this to your wagon so that you can get home and enjoy it while it's hot."

They took the meal out to the wagon and carefully placed the pans so they would travel safely. Cal turned to Liddy. "Thank you. The girls look so proud of themselves, but I'm sure you did most of it," he said in an undertone.

Liddy shook her head. "No, I didn't. They had a hand in it all. I mostly talked them through the steps. I've found it's much easier to remember if one does instead of watches."

Cal helped the girls into the wagon, and they took turns in thanking Liddy for teaching them.

"What will we make tomorrow?" Amy asked.

"Yes, what?" Grace echoed her sister.

Liddy laughed. "I'm not sure. I'll give it some thought tonight."

Cal turned to her once more. "Oh, I forgot to give you extra money for the food. I'm so sorry. I'll get it to you tomorrow."

"Don't worry about it. I—"

"I'll get it to you tomorrow. You plan whatever you want," Cal interrupted her.

Liddy nodded. "I'll keep that in mind."

She waved good-bye to them and went to catch up on her chores before she ate supper. The cow wasn't too happy that she was late with her milking. Liddy promised Bessie that she'd do better the next day.

She went inside, pleased with the accomplishments.

As she ate her meal, she wondered how the McAllister's were enjoying theirs. She knew Cal would make his daughters feel wonderful about the meal they'd helped prepare. She could just imagine the proud and happy looks on their faces that they'd made their father a good supper. Liddy chuckled. A meal that didn't include beans.

After cleaning up the kitchen, she lit the oil lamp and pored over her old cookbook. Luckily, she could teach the girls how to prepare many recipes before they had to learn how to cook those old beans and bacon.

Cal and his girls enjoyed the supper they'd cooked for him. The girls took turns telling him just how they'd done it, and he felt beholden to Liddy, for she'd helped them in a way that made them feel they could repeat the meal on their own.

Amy decided that she wanted a record of the recipes, so she hunted down a piece of brown paper and wrote down the directions Liddy had given them.

Cal helped Grace with the cleanup, while Amy made notes of what she could remember. Then, he gathered all of Liddy's pans together to return them to her the next day.

He lit the lamp and put it on the kitchen table so that the girls could do the schoolwork they usually did while he was cooking supper. They didn't grumble about getting to their lessons late. It seemed as though the cooking classes were worth the delay to them.

Cal settled in his chair by the fire and let peaceful contentment settle over him. He'd had a wonderful meal, and his girls were happy, excited, and looking forward to the next day. The only thing that could make this evening better was a wife to share it all.

Now where did that thought come from?

He knew. It came from the empty spot deep in his heart that had been there since the death of his Mary. She'd been carrying their third child, and it had been a difficult time for her. The baby had come too early. Roswell did have a good doctor, and Cal had rushed to get him. But even he hadn't been able to save either one of them.

The pain had eased through the years, but the loneliness he felt never quite went away. Cal usually just brushed it aside and got on with taking care of his girls.

And that's what he did this time, as he checked their lesson and sent them to get ready for bed. He listened to their prayers and locked up the house before heading to his room. But, as he lay awake in the dark, he couldn't help but wonder if Liddy Evans was as lonely as he was. Was it possible the Lord had brought them together for more than just to help her keep her land?

Cal remembered how pretty she had looked with her face flushed from the warmth of her kitchen, and those little tendrils of hair escaping around her face. Her green eyes sparkled as she'd watched Amy and Grace tell him about their afternoon. The girls liked her a lot, he could tell. And so did he. So did he.

The next few weeks sped by for Liddy. Cal dropped his daughters off right after school and picked them back up as the sun was going down. The girls were easy to teach and fun to be around, and while the evenings and nights were still lonely, Liddy kept herself busy.

She'd made herself one more dress, in a style that could be taken up easily after the baby arrived. Now, she kept herself busy at night by sewing for the baby, baking for Emma's restaurant, and planning the next cooking class for the girls.

School had been dismissed for summer on Friday, and she and Cal had decided that he would bring the girls over right after lunch each day. Liddy was going to teach them a little more about housekeeping than she'd had time for with school in session.

Cal would work his land in the mornings and hers in the afternoons. He had checked out the alfalfa and told her he'd start the first cut in a couple of weeks. It looked to be a good crop. If the next few cuttings over the summer were of the same quality, Liddy wouldn't have to worry about making the rest of the year's payments to Harper.

She was feeling pretty good, except for a few twinges in her back now and again. But it was getting a little more difficult to do the normal daily chores. Gathering eggs was no problem, but she was beginning to wish old Bessie didn't need milking quite so often. Some of the items in her garden would be ready for picking soon, but keeping it clear of weeds was becoming quite a challenge. She was just finishing her weeding chores when she heard a noise. Thinking it was Calvin and the girls, she struggled to her feet and turned to find Douglas Harper standing in the middle of her yard watching her.

Liddy's hand flew to her throat. "Mr. Harper. What are you doing here?"

Chapter 7

I thought I'd come out and see how you are doing, Liddy. I haven't seen you in town lately."

"Since I was able to pay the note ahead by several months, there's been no need for me to come to the bank, Mr. Harper."

He nodded his head and looked around at the alfalfa ripening in the fields. "You've got some good land here, Liddy. But it's too much for a woman to take care of. Farming is a hard, unpredictable life for a man, much less for a woman on her own. It's a struggle you don't need, my dear. My offer still stands."

Liddy felt nauseous at the very thought of his *offer*. "You know that I'm leasing my land to Mr. McAllister. You'll be getting your money on time from now on. There's no need to worry."

Harper nodded. "Leasing might work, as long as you have a good harvest. Nevertheless, you have no control over the elements, my dear. A heavy rain or hailstorm could wipe you out, and take McAllister with you. He won't be able to pay you the rest of what he owes you, if that happens. And you won't be able to make your payments."

Liddy hadn't really thought of the risk Cal was taking. He'd already paid her a deposit. If something happened to both crops, he'd be the real loser, because she'd already paid much of it to the bank.

"She'll make her payments, Harper."

Liddy hadn't heard the approach of Cal's wagon, and the relief she felt as he walked up behind Harper was almost overwhelming.

Harper looked startled to find Cal standing there, but he recovered quickly. "You're guaranteeing that, McAllister?"

"Look around you, man. She's got a bumper crop this year."

Harper nodded. "First cut looks good. But a lot can happen between now and the final cut. I wouldn't count my chickens just yet."

"No, we won't. We'll count on the Lord to get us through. And, unless I'm mistaken, Mrs. Evans paid several months ahead on her loan. She isn't accountable to you until the next payment is due."

Harper held up a hand. "McAllister, you have me all wrong. I've offered to pay off Liddy's loan, myself. Her well-being is of utmost importance to me."

The arrogance of the man sickened Cal. When he'd spotted the man rounding the corner of Liddy's house, he'd hurried his team as fast as he possibly could without alarming the girls.

Not wanting Harper to know how anxious he was that Liddy was here alone with him, Cal had rushed the girls inside and made it to the back of Liddy's house as fast as his long stride could take him. The sight of her with both arms wrapped protectively around her growing middle told him how uncomfortable she was in Harper's presence.

Cal slid a glance toward Liddy and his concern grew. Her eyes were huge and overly bright in a face that was much too pale. Hurrying to her side, he looked down at her. "I think you've been outside in this heat too long, Liddy. The girls are inside. Why don't you go in and rest for a little while?"

Liddy looked from him to Harper and swallowed hard. She met Cal's eyes again and took a deep breath. Then she nodded at him and headed for the house.

"You take care of yourself, Liddy. If you need anything, you just let me know," Harper called after her.

Liddy kept walking.

Cal clinched his fists to his side. *Lord, help me stay in control.* He took another step toward Harper.

"Oh, yes, I think I know how genuine your concern is, Harper. You try to force a woman into marriage just to get control of her land? That kind of concern, she can do without. You can take your leave anytime now, *Mr.* Harper," Cal said.

"Who do you think you are, McAllister? I can call in this loan anytime I want to."

"Mrs. Evans has paid ahead, Harper. It'd be uneth-ical to call in that loan, and you know it."

"Still and all, I *can* do it."

"I wouldn't, if I were you." Cal took a step forward.

He wasn't sure if he was relieved or disappointed when the banker turned and hightailed it out of the yard. Much as he'd have enjoyed the feeling of his fist meeting Harper's chin, he knew it was better this way. No sense in making things harder on Liddy. She still had to pay off the loan. And the faster the better.

He unclenched his fists and watched as Harper drove his team away. He turned to find Amy running toward him.

"Papa! Something is wrong with Mrs. Evans. She's in a lot of pain. Do you think the baby is coming now?"

Cal ran into the house and found Liddy in her rocker. From everything he remembered when the girls were born, he was pretty sure Liddy's time had come. Her eyes tightly closed, she was gripping the arms of the chair, breathing in and out rapidly.

The pain seemed to ease, and her breathing slowed. She opened her eyes and looked at him.

"I think maybe—"

"It's time?" he asked. Liddy nodded at him. "I'll go for the doctor. Do you think you'll be all right? Until I get back?"

Liddy eyes met his, and he could see the fear in them. "I think so. It's a little early, though. Do you think it's really time?"

Cal could tell she needed reassurance, but what did he really know? Babies seemed to have a mind of their own when it came time to be born. He sent up a silent prayer that everything would be all right. But he needed to get the doctor. *Now*, he thought, as he watched another wave of pain wash over Liddy.

"Girls, you help Mrs. Evans to bed and get her as comfortable as possible. I'll be back with the doctor soon as I can."

"Yes, Papa," they both chimed.

Cal was out the door instantly. All the way into town, he prayed that Doc was in and that Liddy and her baby would be fine. If anything happened to them, he'd be looking for Harper. As far as he was concerned, the blame for Liddy's baby coming early rested squarely at the unscrupulous banker's feet.

Cal's prayers were answered, Doc Miller was in, and by nightfall, Liddy was holding her newborn son. Matthew Richard Evans was a little on the small side, but had a robust set of lungs. Doc said Liddy and the baby would be fine.

Emma had followed them out from town, leaving her café in Ben's charge. She would stay the night and several days with Liddy, and no amount of arguing from Liddy was going to change her mind.

Cal was relieved. He didn't want to leave Liddy alone with a newborn baby. He and the girls were allowed in the room after Doc had taken his leave. Liddy was glowing, and although Cal could tell she was exhausted, she looked beautiful with her newborn son in her arms.

"He's a fine, boy, Liddy," Cal said, watching the baby as he curled a tiny finger around his mother's larger one. "You would have made Matthew proud."

"Thank you." Liddy brushed a kiss over her son's forehead and looked back at Cal. "Again. I think I'll be beholden to you for the rest of my life. I'm so glad you were here. I don't know what I'd have done. . ."

"I'm glad I was here, too, Liddy. No need to thank me. You'd have managed."

Liddy chuckled. "Maybe. But Bessie wouldn't have. Thank you for doing my chores, and. . ."

Cal held up his hand. "If I was sick, or down for some reason or another, wouldn't you make sure my girls were taken care of, and my cow milked, and my eggs gathered?"

"Of course, I would."

"Okay, then." Cal could see that Liddy's eyes were starting to droop, and he knew she needed sleep. It'd be only in spurts for a while now, if he remembered right. "I'm going to take the girls home and let you get some rest. If you need anything at all, have Emma let me know. Otherwise, we'll be over tomorrow to check on you all."

Liddy nodded. She knew it would do no good to argue with the man. She let him get halfway out the door before she called, "Thank you, Cal."

He turned and found her eyes closed and her

breathing steady. She looked beautiful sleeping, with her son cuddled close. He wasn't even sure she heard his next words. "You're welcome, Liddy. You did real good. He's a beautiful boy. Sleep well."

Looking back on the past week, Liddy didn't know what she would have done without Emma's help. But, it was Cal's help that had been invaluable.

Being a new mother was intimidating enough, but between Emma's admission that she didn't have a clue what to do, and all the advice given from the wonderful church women bringing food and presents, by the end of the week Liddy had found herself almost in tears.

She'd convinced Emma to go back to her restaurant after five days, thinking she could manage on her own. And she did pretty well until nightfall. Baby Matthew fussed and cried and no amount of rocking, feeding, or changing could quiet him. It was then that she realized the depth of her love for him. Yet, she felt totally inadequate to provide all that he needed. How could she do this alone?

Dear Lord, please help me. I love this child You've blessed me with, but there's so much I don't know, she prayed as she rocked her son in the early morning light. When she heard the light knock on the door, she quickly brushed at her tears and went to open it.

"Liddy, I came to milk Bessie, and the girls insisted on coming to help you out, but I wanted to make sure it would be all right with you."

She hoped he couldn't see she'd been weeping, but her fussing son began to cry in earnest once more, and Liddy couldn't hold her own tears back. She shook her head. "It appears I can use all the help I can get. Obviously, I don't know the first thing about being a mother."

She looked so helpless standing there sobbing, holding her child in her arms, Calvin did the only thing he knew to do. He wrapped his arms around the both of them and led Liddy back to her rocker. He took the baby from her, and went to the door to call his girls in from the wagon.

"Amy, you brew Mrs. Evans a cup of tea like she showed you, and Grace, go find me one of those little soft blankets for the baby, please."

"No, Cal. You've got your own work to see to." Liddy looked up at him as he held her son so easily. "We'll be all right. I'm sorry. We just didn't have a good night—"

"I talked to Emma. She said Matthew hadn't been letting you sleep much, and she knew you were afraid to leave him in her care. . .no more than she knows about babies."

"Oh, dear. Now, I've hurt her feelings."

"No, you haven't. She just wants to make sure it's not too much, you being here all alone." Cal took the blanket Grace brought him and laid it out on the settee. Then he lay the baby down and brought the ends around him, wrapping him snugly. He sat back and jiggled him in his arms until the baby's eyes grew heavy and his lids closed.

Liddy watched closely as she sipped the tea Amy brought her. "How did you do that? Have I been wrapping him too lightly?"

Cal shrugged. "I don't know if there's a right or wrong way to wrap them. This is just the way my girls seemed to be happiest at first. Very snugly wrapped, even in warm weather. I guess it made them feel a little more secure. But I think what Matthew sensed was that I'm not afraid of him."

"And he knows I am?" Liddy couldn't help but chuckle.

"Well, he probably senses that you are unsure of yourself. But you know what, Liddy? I think God gives these instincts to mothers. And I think you just need to listen to them and trust that they come from Him."

"You think so?"

"I do." He brought her sleeping son over to her. "Why don't the two of you go back to bed? Amy and Grace said they'd like to help you, so I'm going to let them gather eggs and put some dinner on for you, if that's all right?"

Liddy let him help her up from the rocker and smiled at his daughters. "Thank you, girls. I'd appreciate your help."

She headed toward her bedroom with the baby. "I don't think I'll sleep long. Wake me if you have any questions."

Cal and his daughters grinned at each other, as Liddy yawned the last sentence.

Liddy slept through the day, rousing only to feed her son when he cried from hunger. She awoke with a start when the setting sun shimmered through her window. The smell of biscuits and stew and the sound of a baby cooing greeted her as she quickly dressed and opened the door. There, sitting in her rocker was Cal, holding Matthew and talking to him as if the baby understood everything he said.

From the way the baby cooed, she wondered if maybe he did.

"It looks like I slept right through lunch. I'm sorry. I—"

"Liddy, you needed the rest. The baby has only been awake for about an hour. We figured you'd be up shortly."

"I'm sure he must be hungry again," Liddy said, taking her son from Cal. "I'll just go feed him."

Cal nodded. "I'll go milk Bessie, and by the time you are finished, the girls will have supper on the table."

Liddy held Matthew close and smiled over at Cal's girls. "It smells delicious. You must give me your recipe."

Amy and Grace giggled at her teasing and began to set the table while she headed for her room.

The baby fell asleep as soon as she fed him, full, clean, and content. Evidently, Cal had bathed and changed him earlier. Liddy wrapped him snugly and put him in the cradle that Cal had brought over for her use. He'd made it for his daughters.

Cal was just washing up from bringing in the milk when she came out of her room. The girls insisted she sit down, and they hurriedly dished up the meal. As Cal said the blessing, Liddy added her own silent prayer, thanking the Lord for bringing this family into her life.

That night marked the change in their routine. Cal and the girls started showing up right after lunch each day. Cal worked her land, the girls learned by helping Liddy, and they all shared the evening meal.

Then, the girls washed dishes while Cal helped Liddy bathe baby Matthew and get him to bed. Only after Liddy was settled in her rocker, with a cup of tea by her side, did they start for home.

Each night, it became harder and harder to see them leave. Amy and Grace had already claimed a spot in her heart. Now, right or wrong, Liddy was sure she was falling more than a little in love with their father.

And where could that possibly lead? Why would any man let himself fall in love with a widow who was in debt? Not to mention one who'd just become a new mother.

Chapter 8

C al wondered just how long he could wait to tell Liddy he loved her and ask for her hand in marriage. It was becoming increasingly difficult to leave her and baby Matthew each night.

Yet, how could he even begin to hope that Liddy might return his feelings when the baby must provide daily reminders of the love she and her husband had shared?

No, he'd best bide his time for now. He loved the woman; there was no denying that fact, and he prayed daily for patience. He'd put his trust in the Lord to let him know when to approach Liddy with a proposal of marriage. He just hoped it would be soon.

First cut of the alfalfa was finished, and it lay drying in the field. Cal hadn't needed any help with the mowing. He'd brought his own horse-drawn mower over the night before, but he had hired several men from town to help rake it into windrows. Tomorrow morning it would be turned, and if the weather held, by that afternoon it would be safely in the barn, out of harm's way.

He had cut his own fields the week before. Liddy and the girls had gone to his house to prepare the noon meal for the men, and today they had done the same at her home.

Now, as he watched them cleaning up after supper, while he entertained the baby, his love for Liddy deepened even more. She was unfailingly patient with his girls, and her son was thriving from her nurturing. She brought the coffeepot over to refill his cup, and bent to kiss her baby's cheek.

Cal wished he had the right to turn her face toward him and bring her lips to his. But he didn't.

"Thank you, Liddy."

"You're welcome." She smiled, and her eyes met his.

He watched a blush steal up her cheeks, and wondered if she'd read his thoughts.

"Thank *you*, Cal. Two months ago, I never thought I'd see those rows of hay in the field. I was sure I was going to lose all of what Matthew and I had worked so hard for. If he could, I know he would thank you for taking such good care of his family and his land."

So that's the way it is. He'd best face the fact that the timing might never be right to ask for Liddy's hand. Now certainly wasn't the right time. It seemed that, in Liddy's eyes, this house he was sitting in, this land he was farming, this child he was holding, and this woman he loved all still belonged to Matthew. Would she always feel that way?

"Liddy, you aren't the only one who's being helped by our arrangement. My girls have learned so much from you, not to mention how they are thriving by the attention you give them. And I stand to make a profit from leasing your land. It's not like I'm doing this all for nothing. The way I see it, we're helping each other." Cal knew his voice sounded rough, but he couldn't help it. He didn't want her gratitude. He wanted her love.

∽⧫∼

Liddy watched Cal's wagon until it was out of sight and sighed deeply. She went inside and bolted the door before easing into her rocker to enjoy her waiting cup of tea. He still made sure she had a fresh-brewed cup before he and the girls left for the night.

Taking a sip of the warm liquid, Liddy leaned back her head and closed her eyes. She'd upset him tonight. She hadn't meant to; she'd only wanted to thank him. She knew he was uncomfortable when she voiced her gratitude, but Liddy couldn't just let him think she took his goodness for granted.

She'd known many Christians, but not all of them acted on their beliefs, like Cal had when he saw to her and her son's needs. He might think he was getting something in return, but Liddy knew who was benefiting the most. And it wasn't Calvin McAllister.

He'd taken a huge risk in leasing her land. She realized that now. If her crop failed, he would be out the money, not her. With the alfalfa already in the field, she hadn't even had to buy seed this year. It looked like they were going to have a good crop, but, still, he was doing all the work.

As far as teaching his girls went, that was a pleasure, and they spent most of their day at her house, helping *her*. Besides, he was giving just as much attention to baby Matthew as she gave to Amy and Grace.

Liddy was sure he went home bone-weary each night, after taking care of both places during the day. Still, he always found time for his girls and to help her with her son. As good a husband as Matthew had been, he hadn't been as considerate of her, after working in the fields all day, as Cal was.

Liddy's heart pounded at her realization. She was in love with Calvin McAllister.

Oh, dear Lord. I did love Matthew. You know I did. But, it's Cal I dream about at night. It's Cal I look forward to seeing each day. What is Your will for us, Father? What am I to do about my feelings for this special man?

Liddy went to bed with no answers, but she trusted the Lord to show her the way.

She was up before dawn, getting her chores out of the way so that she could prepare breakfast for Cal and the men he'd hired to help with the haying. She'd just finished milking Bessie when she heard what sounded like a whip cracking, and her heart fell.

Hurrying outside, she looked up at the sky and saw a flash of lightning. *Oh, dear Lord, not now. Please, keep this storm away until we can get the hay out of the field.*

She hurried to her house, watching the sky closely. This time of year was known for electrical storms. They didn't always have rain in them, but the lightning could be truly ferocious. Huge cloud-to-ground flashes began in earnest, and Liddy hurried in to a crying baby, who had been awakened by the loud booms.

Cal, his girls, and the men he'd hired all showed up at the same time. He rushed Amy and Grace in the house, and against Liddy's protests, he and the men started toward the field to try to save the hay.

Liddy and the children watched from the porch as the storm moved closer. She prayed silently, all the while, for Cal and the men to be safe, as she watched them hurry to load the hay into wagons.

Normally, it would be turned over and allowed to lay in the field until the afternoon. But with the storm approaching, it appeared that Cal had decided to get it into the barn as fast as possible.

Less than half the field's yield had been moved to the barn, when a huge bolt struck the field. Immediately, a row of hay ignited, the flames shooting down the row and across to the next.

Liddy quickly handed the baby to Amy and ran out to the barn. She gathered all of the burlap bags she could find and rushed to wet them in the watering trough.

Cal met her at the edge of the field and took them from her. "Stay here. I don't know that we'll be able to do much, but if it should come close to the house, you'll need to get what you can and get the children in the wagon."

Several other ranchers who'd seen the flames had joined in the fight. Some started digging a trench to keep the house and barn safe, while others were filling buckets from the water trough, and everyone was doing all they could to help. But there was no rain with this storm, and Liddy knew saving the crop was a losing battle. By the time the men had the fire under control, there wasn't much left of the crop to save. Their hopes for a good first cut were gone.

Liddy brushed at the tears running down her face as Cal approached, his own face sooty from fighting the fire.

He gathered her in his arms. "I'm sorry, Liddy."

She shook her head. "There's no more you could do, Cal. It's not your fault."

"I should have cut earlier."

"You had no way of knowing this was going to happen. It'll grow again. There'll be another cut."

Cal nodded and brushed her still-wet cheek.

"I'll have some breakfast for everyone shortly," Liddy said.

"You don't need to do that, Liddy. No one expects—"

"It'll keep me busy, Cal."

He nodded. "Ring the bell when you're ready."

Liddy and the girls were cleaning up after feeding the

men who'd come to help. The storm had moved out of the vicinity, but someone had mentioned that they'd heard there'd been some hail toward Cal's place, and he and several of the men went to see if the reports were true.

Matthew was down for a nap and the girls were trying to be quiet. Liddy sent them to gather eggs and check on Bessie.

She prayed there hadn't been any damage to Cal's crops and thanked the Lord that, as bad as it seemed at the moment, they had managed to save some of the hay. Most importantly to her, Cal and the other men had been unharmed as they fought the fire.

She hated that he blamed himself. There was no way he could have known the storm would build up. Things like this happened.

Liddy poured herself a cup of tea, but found she couldn't sit still, and decided to go help Amy and Grace in the barn. But when she opened the door, it was to find Douglas Harper at the bottom of the steps. Her heart plummeted before seeming to stop.

"My dear Liddy, I heard in town about your misfortune and had to come see for myself. I'm so sorry about your crop."

How dare the man? She'd had about all of his sarcastic lying that she could take. Loan or no loan, she wasn't taking that kind of attitude from this man anymore.

"I'd appreciate your getting off my land, Harper."

The man didn't deserve to be called *Mr.*, and Liddy couldn't bring herself to do so. She wanted to run, but she stood firm, as Harper took a step up.

"Whose land, my dear? I think you are mistaken in calling it yours. Because, you see, I'm calling in your note. With no crop, there is no way you can pay your next installment. And I've given you all the leeway I can."

"I'm paid up. And the next payment isn't due for two more weeks."

"Doesn't matter. You won't have the money then."

Liddy lifted her chin a notch higher. "I may."

Little Matthew had awakened and could be heard crying from inside the house. She headed back through the door but turned to Harper once more. "I don't have time to discuss this with you right now. My son needs me. You'll excuse me if I go see to him."

She went inside and shut the door, hurrying to pick up Matthew. She wouldn't rest easy until she knew Harper was off her property. The girls were in the barn, and she didn't want them to be frightened by his presence.

But when she turned, it was to find that Harper had followed her inside.

"Liddy, my dear. You have me all wrong," he said coming toward her. "My offer still stands. I'd like nothing more than to take care of you and your son. If you'll marry me, you'll never have to worry about paying off your loan."

She gathered her son close. "Get out of my house, Harper. You know your so-called *offer* repulses me. I'll lose my house and land before I'd marry you!"

"And that's exactly what you'll be doing, if you say no. I will call in the note tomorrow." He advanced toward her.

"Harper." There was no sweeter sound to Liddy's ears than that of Calvin's voice as he entered the house.

"Ah, McAllister." Harper turned to face Cal. "I should have known you'd be showing up. I figured there was something going on between the two of you. Well, you can't help Mrs. Evans this time, because I'm calling in her note first thing tomorrow."

"No, you are not." Cal was across the room in two strides and had the banker by the collar. "And you will apologize for speaking to my fiancée that way. *Now.*"

Liddy felt as if her heart somersaulted all the way to her feet and back. What was Cal doing?

"Your what? Did you say fiancée?" Harper turned first to Cal, and then back to Liddy. "Is this true?"

"I. . ." Liddy was at a loss for words.

Cal had no such problem. "Harper, we don't owe you any explanations. All you need to know is that Liddy and I will be in first thing tomorrow morning to pay off her debt. No. Better yet, we'll be in your office by closing time today."

He gave the man a shake before letting go of his collar. "Now, apologize nicely, and get out of this house and off the property."

"I'm sorry, Mrs. Evans," Harper said sarcastically as he turned and headed for the door. But he tried to get in the last word. "You be there. Or I will have the sheriff deliver foreclosure papers. And I'll have you arrested for accosting me, McAllister."

With that, Harper slammed out the door.

Cal followed him and called, "Well, you can try, but I don't think the sheriff will do your bidding, once he hears how you tried to blackmail a widow into marrying you."

He watched until the banker was safely off the property before turning back to Liddy.

As soon as Harper had gone out the door, she'd dropped into her rocker, holding her son securely in her lap. She was trembling like a leaf. What had Cal been thinking to tell Harper such a thing?

"Liddy?"

She looked up to find Cal smiling down at her. "Calvin McAllister. What have you done? What are we going to do now?"

Cal lowered himself to one knee in front of her. "If you'll have me, we're going to get married."

"Calvin, you can't marry me just to get me out of debt. And the crop is nearly gone anyway. There is no money."

"Remember, I told you I had a good crop last year? Well, I'm doing fine, Liddy. I have more than enough to pay off your loan to Harper. I don't want him spreading talk about you, Liddy. And he will if we don't get married. You know that."

Tears welled up in her eyes. This was what she wanted, but it was happening for all the wrong reasons. "Cal, you can't marry me to protect my reputation, either. And I don't want your pity."

Cal lifted her chin, so that her eyes met his. "Look at me, Liddy. Pity is *not* what I feel for you. And it's not what you see in my eyes. What you see there is love, Liddy. Pure and simple love.

"I know I've done this all wrong," Cal continued. "I meant to give you more time to get over losing Matthew. But, Liddy, if there's even a chance that, one day, you could learn to love me, I'll settle for that. I promise I'll try to be a good husband to you, and father to young Matthew."

"Shh. . .shh," she said, her fingers coming up to still his words. Her heart sang with the realization that Calvin did love her. She had never known this man to lie, and she knew he wouldn't lie to her about something as important as this.

"I've been falling in love with you for weeks, Calvin McAllister. If you mean what you say, then my answer is *yes*. I'll marry you. And I'll happily spend the rest of my days trying to be a good wife to you and mother to our children. Yours, mine, and ours, if the good Lord wills it."

Cal lifted her fingers from his lips and kissed her palm. Standing, he pulled Liddy and her son into his embrace and hugged them tightly.

Tipping her chin, he lowered his lips to hers and captured them in the kiss he'd only dreamed of until now. Tentative at first, he deepened the kiss to seal the promise of their love for each other.

It was still light when they returned from town. They had to go from one bank to the other, but before the afternoon was over, Liddy and Cal left Harper's bank with her note stamped paid in full and the knowledge that he would never be able to take her place away from her.

They celebrated with supper at Emma's. Once she found out they were going to be married, nothing would do her but to help plan the wedding.

By the time Cal pulled his wagon into Liddy's yard, there were only a few hot spots still smoldering in the field.

Thrilled that Matthew would soon be their baby brother, Amy and Grace happily took him inside, while Cal and Liddy walked hand in hand to the edge of the field.

Liddy sent up a silent prayer of thanksgiving—thanking God that only the crop had burned, that the Lord had kept Cal safe, and that His will for her and Cal and their children was for them to become a family.

Cal turned her to him and wrapped his arms around her. "You know, if this field hadn't caught on fire today, I'd probably still be wondering how much longer I needed to wait until I could ask you to marry me. But

I think the Lord had plans for us all along, even before you agreed to let me lease your land."

Loving the feel of being in the circle of Cal's arms, Liddy smiled and nodded. "He planted the seeds of love in each of our hearts, when all we thought we were doing was helping each other out."

"We'll harvest this field over and over again," Cal said. "But the Lord intends for our love to last through all the harvests of our lives. I love you, Liddy, today, tomorrow, and forever." Cal bent his head toward her.

Their lips met, and the lingering kiss they shared convinced Liddy that Calvin McAllister did indeed love her. . .every bit as much as she loved him.

JANET LEE BARTON

Born in New Mexico, Janet has lived all over the South, but she and her husband plan to stay put in southern Mississippi where they have made their home for the past six years. With three daughters and six grandchildren between them, they feel blessed to have at least one daughter, Nicole, her husband Darren, and two precious granddaughters, Mariah and Paige, living in the same town. Janet loves being able to share her faith through her writing. Happily married to her very own hero, she is ever thankful that the Lord brought Dan into her life, and she wants to write stories that show that the love between a man and a woman is at its best when the relationship is built with God at the center. She's very happy that the kind of romances the Lord has called her to write can be read by and shared with women of all ages, from teenagers to grandmothers alike.

The Applesauce War

by Ellen Edwards Kennedy

Chapter 1

New York State, September, 1901

Verity McCracken swallowed the bite of pancake she'd been chewing and frowned at her father over the breakfast table. "I don't believe it. You're saying that you and Mr. Delorme aren't speaking? You've been friends all your lives. Why now?"

Jacob McCracken poured more of his homemade maple syrup over the already sodden pancakes and stared intently at the mess. "Druther not talk about it." He dropped his fork and crossed his arms over his chest. "Just please do what I ask." His salt-and-pepper eyebrows dipped ominously over his pale blue eyes.

Verity looked over at the big, black, wood-burning stove where her mother stood. "Are you mad at the Delormes, too?"

Grace McCracken rolled her eyes, then turned towards the stove, and wrapped a dishtowel around the handle of the steaming coffeepot. "Don't bring me into this!" Hefting the pot, she filled the cups around the table, her husband's, her own, Verity's.

"But why? What caused this?"

Grace smiled down at her only chick. "I'm sure I couldn't say," she said, "But if y'ask me, it's all a lot of applesauce," she added with a meaningful glance at her husband.

Jacob didn't meet his wife's eyes. "Now there's another thing 'at gets my goat!" he said, returning to his breakfast with clumsy enthusiasm. "Why are people always sayin' something's 'applesauce,' as if it was of no account?" He pointed at the ever-present bowl of the stuff. "Applesauce is good for you—and dee-licious!" He spooned a large dollop on his plate for emphasis.

"Papa, it's just an expression. It doesn't reflect on your apples." Verity had to smile.

Jacob caught her at it. "This is no laughing matter, Missy. I'm dead serious."

Verity immediately sobered and her heart sank. Papa wasn't joking, as he frequently did. Whatever difference stood between Papa and Gerard Delorme, it would have to be important. Yet Mama seemed to take it in stride. The situation was all very puzzling. Especially the part about Gerard Delorme's youngest son.

"What's Pete done? Why are you mad at him, too?"

Jacob's face remained screwed up tightly. "I never asked much of my only daughter, just this one thing," he told the cream pitcher. He looked over at Verity.

"Are you going to mind me, girl?"

"You mean to stay away from Pete? I don't know, Papa; after all, it's not my fight. Besides, Pete's away at college. I haven't laid eyes on him since Christmas and that's—what?—nine months, at least. And we were never really that close."

Verity turned to her mother. "I'm going to the mercantile today. I might see one of the Delormes on the street. You want me to ignore them?"

Grace sat down at the table. "No, siree, we don't!" she said, frowning at Jacob as she stirred her coffee. "You were raised to be a lady and a lady you shall be!" She tapped the drops off her spoon and took a sip. "No matter what anybody says." She took another. The law had been laid down.

"O' course I want you to be polite," said Jacob, slightly chastened. "Just no. . .lollygagging, understand?"

Verity drew herself up straight in her chair. "Papa, I have never 'lollygagged' in my life," she said frostily, "though I never did know what that word meant."

Jacob drained his coffee. "You know perzactly what I mean, though, Missy." He glanced at the old school clock on the kitchen wall. "Six thirty-five already—I'm burnin' daylight! Got chores to do." He bent to kiss his daughter, then his wife. "Don't forget my peppermints," he reminded Verity, then clapped on his hat and was out the back door.

Having already milked six cows before breakfast, Jacob would usually be inspecting the state of his apples in his thousand-tree orchard, or, in the company of his lone hired hand, Fred, chopping the weeds from an autumn crop of cabbages. Time was of the essence this far north in a valley of the old York State's Adirondack region. Cold weather came on fast once the leaves started turning, and it was only a week before the all-important apple harvest. But today, Jacob had more pressing matters to tend to and an appointment to keep.

The newly risen autumn sun caused him to squint as he walked briskly between the rows of low-hanging apple trees to the narrow strip where his land bordered Gerard Delorme's. There was a stone wall there, with a wild raspberry bush nearby and a three-step stile that he climbed over with long-accustomed ease.

There, while watching Delorme's calm Guernseys grazing, he leaned against the stone wall, pulled a crisp apple from his pocket, and thought about his daughter's future as he munched.

A hand slapped his shoulder roughly. "Well met, Jacob McCracken!" Gerard Delorme had come down the path along the fence instead of across the pasture, as expected. " 'In thy face I see the map of honor, truth, and loyalty.' "

Jacob swallowed, then grinned. "What's that, Gerry? More Shakespeare? My pa allus said you'd spoil your eyes with all that readin'."

"*Henry the Sixth,* act 3," admitted Gerard, "but if you don't want to associate with bookworms, you'd best look to your own household. I hear Verity took high honors at Plattsburgh Normal School."

Jacob blushed with pride even as he shrugged away the compliment to his daughter. "It's true, but we don't mention it much. Can't have her gettin' the big head."

Suddenly, Gerard's expression changed. He looked over each shoulder. "Did you do it?" he asked eagerly.

Jacob regarded his apple core thoughtfully, then tossed it into the bushes. "Ayah, but I didn't like it much."

"No more than I. When I told my family this morning, they all thought I had lost my sanity."

Jacob shielded his eyes with his hand and stared out at the Delorme dairy herd. "Nothin' they didn't know already."

"Very funny. What did you give as a reason?"

"Didn't give none. Refused to discuss it."

Gerard threw back his head and laughed heartily. "Well done! That's exactly the tack I took! Two great minds with but a single thought!"

Jacob shrugged. "That's mighty nice talking and all, but I dunno if this thing's gonna work. My wife—"

"You told her?" Gerard's brown button eyes widened.

"O' course. But she's promised to keep mum."

Gerard sighed. "Good." He slapped Jacob's back. "Fear not! It's a masterful plan and can only lead to—"

"Gerry, I don't understand why we just can't tell them we'd like 'em to keep company and get married someday."

"Kiss of death, Jacob, kiss of death! Could anything

be less romantic than a match arranged by Mother and Father? Certainly not!"

"I guess I see what you mean. They are pretty bull-headed kids, but maybe nature will just. . .take its course. They'll be at the barn dance at your place next month and they'll see each other around town. . . ."

"We can't chance it. Your daughter and my son are attractive young people. What if they found somebody else in the meantime? Disaster!"

"But—"

"It'll be the romantic story of the Montagues and Capulets all over again. The Bard's immortal tale. What could be more enticing than forbidden love?" When he smiled, Gerard's plump cheeks resembled the round, red McIntoshes hanging from Jacob's trees.

"But didn't that Romeo and Juliet thing end up kinda sad?"

"That's because the families were really feuding! As soon as we see Cupid's arrow fly, we reconcile, bury the hatchet, smoke the peace pipe, and all's well that ends well!"

Jacob took off his hat and scratched his head. "Well, I guess so. We've already got the ball rolling. So what do we do now?"

"Just watch that ball roll, Jacob! You said your girl will be in town on errands today? Well, so will my son. He begins his legal career reading law with Ted Essex's firm this very morning." He looked at the sky. "When shall we meet again? In thunder, lightning, or in rain?"

Jacob was puzzled. "What's the weather got to do with it?"

Gerard sighed. "Just a quoting from *Macbeth*, act 1, scene 1."

"Well, rain or shine, I'll be here tomorrow at the same time. I hope this thing works out." Jacob replaced his hat on his head.

Gerard grasped his friend's hand firmly. "It will, I assure you. Perhaps before too many more autumns, we'll be calling each other *'Grandpere.'*"

Jacob chuckled as he shook Gerard's hand. "Hmm, Grandpa. Sounds pretty good. If that happens, it'll be worth every smidgen of this foolishness!"

Chapter 2

In her absentmindedness, Verity overlooked two newly laid eggs during her trip to the henhouse. Then, she scattered far more feed corn than was necessary, to the chickens' frantic delight.

"Verity," Grace asked as her daughter meandered through the kitchen, lost in thought, "what happened to the leftover bacon?"

"What? Oh." Verity looked down at the empty platter sitting by the sink, waiting to be washed. "I guess I put it in the dog's dish with the leftover pancakes."

Grace sighed as she pumped water into the sink. "Well, it's gone now. I was going to add it to the beans." She nodded towards a large pot simmering on the back of the stove.

"I'm sorry, Mama. I was thinking of something else." Verity turned her head, scanning the kitchen. "Where's the dishtowel I just had in my hand?"

Her mother ran a soapy dishrag around the rim of a coffee cup. "Hangin' over your shoulder." She dipped the cup in the steaming rinse water and handed it over. "Punkin, you better get your head on straighter than your hat before you go into town. Can't have you coming home with a big sack of salt instead of flour!" She smiled, wiped one hand on her apron, and pushed a shiny brown curl from Verity's forehead. "And quit frettin' over this thing with the Delormes. It'll all come out in the wash."

" 'Come out in the wash.' What does that mean, exactly?" Verity had learned in college that it was important to define one's terms.

"I can't say any more."

Verity began to feel angry. First, Papa's weird statement at breakfast and now Mama talking in riddles! "But this quarrel or whatever it is—what about forgiveness? Is this falling-out so bad they can't forgive each other? It's not Christian!" Verity waved her hand in the air dramatically. The damp coffee cup in her fingers flew across the kitchen and shattered against a pine cupboard.

"Oh! Oh! Mama! I'm so sorry!" She dashed over, knelt, and began picking up the shards. "Oh, it's ruined! Your cup!"

Her mother patted her shoulder. "Run along. You'll cut yourself; you're that addlepated this morning. It's not my best china." She took the fragments from her daughter's hand. "Go on; get dressed for town. There's a nice shirtwaist in your cabinet, and wear that straw hat with the bow. You looked so pretty in it when you stepped off the train."

Nodding gratefully, Verity fled.

"Poor mite. This thing has got her in such a dither," muttered Grace as she swept the remains of the cup into a dustpan.

Verity's hands shook as she unbraided her long hair. Being a full-grown woman of nineteen required that she wear her hair up, but sometimes the effort was just more trouble than it was worth. "I miss being ten," she told the mirror. "I could wear boy's overalls and braids and climb trees, and Papa and Mama acted like normal parents."

Bending forward, she gave her brown mane several long, downward strokes with the hairbrush. Then, she placed a little rectangular pillow, curiously called a "rat," on the top of her head, lifted her hair over it, and fastened the ends in a coil at the base of her neck with the half-dozen U-shaped hairpins she held between her lips. With satisfaction, Verity surveyed her result in the mirror. The rat gave her silky hair fullness on top, as fashion dictated.

"What to do?" She asked herself as she buttoned up her shirtwaist. "I didn't promise Papa anything, really," she mused as she pulled the shoe buttons through their buttonholes with the long metal hook. "I'll just have to play things by ear," she decided as she fastened her fashionable new hat to her hair with a wicked-looking, six-inch hatpin. Not that she had need for them in Enfield, but her friends at college had reminded her that hatpins could serve as more than decoration on a long train journey or in a big city like Albany.

As she climbed into the wagon, Verity remembered the last sermon she had heard in the college chapel, on the Ten Commandments. " 'Honor thy father and thy mother: that thy days may be long upon the land,' " she quoted aloud over the back of the two old reliable grays, Thunder and Lightning.

Thunder stamped impatiently until Verity clucked at the horses and jiggled the reins. "Giddap."

Papa was right about one thing. He'd been a re-markably indulgent father, asking little of her, only the standard daily chores, and the respect due him as her parent. Never once had he discouraged her dream of going to normal school. He'd even dipped into the family savings for the tuition and had pressed a five-dollar bill into her gloved hand as she boarded the train. "For some silly girl thing or 'nother," he'd whispered and kissed her cheek.

Verity dabbed a tear off that same cheek with the back of her glove. It was the least she could do, respect her father's wishes, and steer clear of the Delormes as much as possible. Given time, the thing, whatever it was, would probably heal itself. Verity sat up, whispered a prayer, and resolutely turned her mind to town and the items on her mother's list.

❧

Pierre Delorme, better known as Pete to the people of Enfield, New York, and the surrounding countryside, was having much the same debate with himself as he sat at a desk in the office of Essex and Westcloth, Esquires, Attorneys at Law.

"Reading law," meant serving as an apprentice in a law firm. Before him lay the daunting task of researching and reviewing a complicated legal precedent for his employers. He had done everything in preparation: gathered a healthy stack of paper, sharpened six pencils into the metal wastebasket with his penknife and even pulled down several relevant volumes from the walls of the firm's copious law library.

Now, all that remained was for him to crack open a book and get busy, but his mind simply wouldn't focus. It didn't bode well for his first day of employment.

Pete picked up a pencil and wrote a heading, *What are the central points at issue?* Then he underlined it three times.

Good question, he thought.

What on earth had gotten into Father this morning? Breakfast had been exceedingly strange: the astonishing little speech, delivered with many long words and trite expressions; Mother, crying quietly into her napkin; David and Anne exchanging shocked looks and even Nancy, the cook, pretending to be deaf as she carried in the tray of sausages.

"But why?" his brother, David, had demanded. "What have the McCrackens done?"

"I have spoken," said Gerard. "There will be no further discussion."

And there wasn't. Although David's wife, Anne, was unable to finish her oatmeal and begged, in a whisper, to be excused from the table long before the meal was over.

Mother had stopped him in the dark front hall as he left for town. "Oh, Pierre, please say a prayer for your father!" she whispered as she dabbed her eye with a delicate lace handkerchief, "I truly think he has lost his mind! He refuses to say another word, only forbids us all—forbids! Did you hear him use that word?—Forbids us to have any truck whatsoever with the Mc-Crackens." She blew her nose and gazed up at him. "Our dear friends! How can he do this?"

Pete looked down fondly into the wide eyes of his dainty blond mother. "I don't know, but Father has always been good to us and I guess we'll just have to trust that this thing is important to him. It'd have to be." He kissed her forehead. "We'll both pray, Mother, and everything will turn out all right. I know it."

Marie Delorme threw her arms around her youngest son, the child most like herself at heart. "Thank you, dear, and now go do your best work for Mr. Essex. We're so proud of you! I know you'll make a splendid lawyer."

❧

Pete jolted from his reverie when his pencil point broke with a loud snap. He had been pressing too hard. He picked up another and tried to return to his task.

. . .*the central points at issue.* . .

He made a decision. He loved his father and Pete would do as he asked, have little or nothing to do with anyone of the McCracken clan. It was a pity, though. He'd heard that Verity had finished school and was back to stay. Rumor was, she was prettier than ever, and he'd have liked to have seen for himself.

Pete blinked hard and took a deep breath. Better tackle the task at hand before Messrs. Essex and Westcloth decided they had no need of such a lazy law clerk. "Let's see now. . ." He opened a volume and began to turn the pages.

Verity completed her shopping far earlier than she expected.

"That's the last of it," said Mr. Bernard, as he hefted a huge sack of flour into the back of the wagon. "You sure you don't want me to pull down those bolts of new gingham my missus ordered? It just come in, and if I say so myself, the colors are pretty as a picture!" The merchant smiled broadly. "You've got enough time to run up a new dress for the barn dance next month!"

Verity hadn't the heart to tell him that gingham was no longer in fashion among college girls. She smiled. "Perhaps another day," she said, surveying the main street for familiar faces. She hadn't spotted a single Delorme so far this morning, and she felt vaguely disappointed.

She was about to accept Mr. Bernard's help in climbing aboard when her eyes fell on the sign for the Carnegie Library across the village park. The lending library had been a favorite spot of hers before she went away to college. A nice book would take her mind off the strange happenings at home.

"If I may," she told the storekeeper, "I'll leave the wagon here for just a bit." It could be done in a small town like Enfield. In a larger city, someone might steal her cargo.

"Verity McCracken!" said Verna Reilly, the librarian. "Back from Plattsburgh Normal School, a full-fledged teacher, I hear!"

"We'll find out when school starts," said Verity modestly as she shook the elderly woman's hand. "In the city, they start much earlier, you know."

"Oh, but the children are needed to help with the harvest, dear," Miss Reilly reminded her. " 'Happy is the man that hath his quiver full of them,' " she added, quoting Psalms. "Every hand is needed." She took a long look at Verity. "I must say, I really like that hat! Very becoming!"

Verity looked around the dear, familiar little library. The building had been the post office in years past, but when Enfield's fortunes had turned the village into a town, the post office had moved to larger quarters. Volunteers had torn out the old fixtures and replaced them with bookshelves, tables, and chairs; and the Carnegie Foundation had supplied the funds for the purchase of books.

Miss Reilly clapped her hands. "But, of course, you've come for something to read. I remember you liked Dickens. Have you read *A Tale of Two Cities*? It's about the French Revolution, and it's just thrilling." She pointed as she resumed her seat at the reception desk. "You know where everything is. Just make yourself at home, my dear."

Miss Reilly's suggestion appealed to Verity. It was one of the few Dickens' books she had not yet read. The turmoil of the French Revolution might prove a welcome change from the present unnerving situation. She made her way into the stacks—*or stack*, she pointed out to herself as she humorously compared this little one-room establishment to the massive collection of volumes available in the college library. She pulled out the book in question and turned to the first page. "It was the best of times, it was the worst of times—" she read the first line to herself in a whisper.

"Why, Pete Delorme!" she heard Miss Reilly say, "here you are, back from college, big as life!"

Verity stiffened.

"And what a coincidence! I believe we have a friend of yours here," the little lady added merrily.

Chapter 3

Verity hugged *A Tale of Two Cities* to her chest and listened.

"Really?" There was cheerfulness and amusement in Pete's deep, familiar voice. "Who is it?"

Could the feud be all in Papa's head, or a misunderstanding, perhaps? Oh, let it be so!

"Miss Verity McCracken, fresh from normal school," Miss Reilly announced gaily.

Verity held her breath.

Silence.

"Oh, Verity," Miss Reilly sang out, "would you come out here, please? I don't think Mr. Delorme believes me."

Verity sighed deeply and stepped from behind the bookshelf, holding the book to herself like armor. Her fears were confirmed when she saw Pete's face: lips compressed, eyes elusive, hands unconsciously thrust in his pockets.

"Good day, Mr. Delorme," said Verity stiffly, offering her gloved hand.

"Miss McCracken," he responded, looking intently at the hem of her gown. His grip was weak, and he released her hand as quickly as though he held a poisonous snake.

Verity felt a prickle of tears forming in her eyes. Why was she suddenly feeling so desolate?

"Excuse me, please," he said, and stepped around her. After a brief, stricken glance at her face, he disappeared behind a bookshelf.

"Um, well. . ." Miss Reilly, feeling the chill in the air, hastened to smooth things. "Did you wish to check out that book, dear?"

Verity looked down at the volume she held tightly against her chest. "Er, yes, thank you," she said, and was surprised that her voice sounded so weak.

"An excellent choice!" said Miss Reilly as she picked up a pencil, opened the long ledger book, and began the tedious task of recording Verity's choice. Carefully, she recorded Verity's name and the title and author of the book she had chosen. With infuriating slowness, she consulted a wall calendar that bore the picture of a kitten and promoted the virtues of a patent medicine. "Is one week time enough, dear?"

"Of course," Verity said, more sharply than she had intended. She felt dizzy. She needed air.

A book slammed to the floor in the back of the library.

Verity flinched.

"Oops, sorry," said Pete.

Verity remembered Pete saying those words before. Five years ago, at a hayride, when he and another boy had burrowed under the hay and popped up here and there, causing squeals among the girls. He had been a smart-aleck pest back then, with a rebellious yellow cowlick sticking up in the back of his head, full of himself and his newly grown height. The older girls had liked him, of course, but fourteen-year-old Verity was determined not to waste her time with boys. She would get an education first.

And she had, she reminded herself, trying not to think about the long, cozy evenings in the dormitory, where she and her friends had shared their dreams and Verity had verbally sketched her idea of the Perfect Man: tall, strong, pious, articulate, a bibliophile. And a person well-read enough to know the meaning of the word.

"Here you are, my dear," said Miss Reilly, handing the book back to her.

Verity made a courteous good-bye and hurried to the waiting farm wagon.

❦

Pete heard the library door closing and realized he'd been standing stock-still, his fists constricted painfully. The fallen book lay splayed at his feet.

An image of Verity McCracken obscured the wall of books before him: not too tall; a halo of shiny brown hair around a pale, oval face; a delicate pink mouth, clamped into a thin line as she extended her hand—so tiny, that hand—and a silvery line of tears forming along the bottom of wide, pale-blue eyes. She was trembling as she stood there; he had sensed it rather than seen it.

So, it was true. The feud was real, and Verity Mc-Cracken, as any loyal daughter should, was observing her father's wishes.

An anathema, Pete thought, *I'm anathema to her.* He was rather proud that the Latin word had occurred to him. *I am cursed, excommunicated, taboo, as far as Verity McCracken is concerned.* He wondered at the pang he felt at the thought.

Verity's just one of the hometown girls, he reminded himself, and she had always been a terrible snob, even as a kid. Never kept company with any of the Enfield boys. Not like the girls who had flocked around him in high school, eager to kiss any fellow who asked them; who thought reading a book was a waste of time.

Pete shook his head and picked up the fallen book. A nice, smart girl. And he was duty-bound to have nothing to do with her.

⚜

"Arrrgh!" Verity kicked the huge sack of flour. A hole opened in its side and a little spilled out onto the dirt of the country road. "Oh, no!" She collapsed on top of the huge bag. Things were going from bad to worse.

When the wagon, improperly balanced, began to run into a roadside rut, it had only seemed sensible to stop and rearrange the cargo in the buckboard. With all her strength, she had tugged the sack of flour over to prop it against one side. She intended to balance its weight by rolling the keg of nails to the other, but the heel of her shoe had caught in the hem of her skirt, and both Verity and the flour had tumbled over the side.

She had been fortunate—she could have broken her neck—still, it was difficult to feel thankful. Her twisted ankle was beginning to throb and small white clouds of flour were being carried off in the late summer breeze. She knelt, pulled out her long hatpin, and used it to fasten the edges of the flour bag together. As she sat back to survey her handiwork, her pretty new straw hat, its black velvet ribbon flapping, flew off her head. She crawled after it, only to have a sudden gust roll it a good twenty feet away. She sat back and only just caught herself from giving the flour sack another pounding in her frustration.

"What do I do now?" she asked Thunder, who stood patiently observing over his massive gray flank this strange behavior, while Lightning, as usual, remained oblivious. "Do I leave it?"

Verity knew that horses couldn't shrug, but Thunder's expression carried much the same sentiment as he gazed at her. She stood and leaned against the horse's expansive middle, taking comfort from his strength. She consulted the tiny brooch watch that had been her graduation present from her parents. It was after four o'clock already. Someone should be coming along the road pretty soon. Surely they'd give her a hand with the huge sack. It was simply too wasteful to leave it. Besides, her mother was nearly out of flour.

Pete Delorme was proud of himself. In spite of many challenging diversions, he'd given his employers a good day's work, and Mr. Essex had been pleased with this progress.

He smiled as his horse, Sandy, cantered gently. There was no hurry. Dinner wouldn't be for another hour and a half. He'd have time for a talk with his father. It was imperative that he get to the bottom of this outrageous situation with the McCrackens. His mind returned to the scene in the library, and he experienced a heavy sadness. It was ridiculous. He had no quarrel with Verity McCracken, and he was eager to reestablish acquaintance with her. Very eager indeed. But what could be done about it?

He spotted the hat first, skittering along the road in a brisk breeze. It looked familiar and in need of rescue, but before he could dismount and retrieve it, the straw skimmer with the charming black velvet bow rolled away among the forlorn stumps of a harvested cornfield to his right.

Where had that come from?

He rounded a curve in the road and saw a wagon and horses ahead. He urged Sandy forward and narrowly missed trampling a gigantic sack of flour.

Where was the driver? He looked at the horses, and with a sickening lurch, recognized them.

McCracken horses! Verity had been driving this

wagon. Where was she? Hurt? Kidnapped? He dismounted and called frantically, "Miss McCracken! Verity! Are you all right?"

"Here," he heard a faint call from beneath a roadside tree.

Hastily fastening Sandy's reins to the wagon, he jogged over to where Verity was struggling to stand.

"I'm so sorry," she said as she brushed grass from her skirt; "I must have fallen asleep." She looked up at him, froze for a split second, then said breathlessly, "Oh, it's you, Mr. Delorme! I am so. . .glad to see you." She was hatless and disheveled. Strands of hair had fallen out of her chignon and straggled down her back. There was a smudge of flour across her forehead. "I really am," she added.

It seemed to Pete that a golden glow began to fill the landscape, though the hour was long before sunset. He gave her his arm, which she took without hesitation, and they stepped carefully among the rocks and fallen branches, making their way back to the road where the three horses and the wagon waited.

"How did this happen?" laughed Pete when Verity stopped and stood balefully beside the fallen flour sack.

Laughing at herself, she explained in vivid detail, with a range of gestures and a lively vocabulary that astonished him. Especially touching was the sight of the attempted repair of the hole with a hatpin.

"And that's how you lost your poor hat," he finished for her with a chuckle as he removed his suit jacket and handed it to her. Rolling up his sleeves, he hunched up under the weight of the enormous sack and heaved it aboard the wagon in one groaning motion.

"Oh, my," Verity's eyes were huge. "I could have never done that. I am most obliged to you."

He helped her into the wagon. "It was nothing, honestly," he said, sudden bashfulness sweeping over him. Then, he brightened. "I think I know where your hat is, too!"

"Oh, I couldn't let you—" she began, but he was already dashing down the road and across the uneven cornfield. The deed of capturing the hat took only a minute, but the rush of pleasure he experienced as he finally brandished his trophy amazed him.

Verity clapped her hands in delight and received the prize with solicitous tenderness, sweeping away crumbs of dirt with delicate fingertips. "Oh, Pete—Mr. Delorme—I'm so grateful to you. . ." As she handed his jacket down to him from her perch on the wagon, her blue gaze was all he could see.

He stumbled on the words, but he was determined to get them out. "I—am—just—so—sorry."

No explanation was necessary.

"No—you—I mean—" She shook her head violently and a tear flew out of one eye. "I just wish I knew what it was about."

"So do I!" he said with amazement.

"You mean you don't know, either?"

"No!"

They shared a laughing moment of bewilderment, then, "May I drive you home?" Pete asked shyly.

She gestured to the seat beside her. "Please do." Her lips were drawn up in a gently curved bow.

As they drove, ever so slowly, toward the McCracken farm, they discussed the extraordinary mornings they each had experienced and marveled at the remarkable similarity.

"What's going to happen?" Verity asked as they neared the turnoff to her home.

Pete shook his head. "I don't know. But something's got to be done; that's certain."

"Absolutely."

"Would you—I mean—could we, um, pray about it?"

"Oh, yes," said Verity eagerly. "Please."

Together, they bowed their heads and prayed, in turn, for understanding, for peace, for resolution. When they raised them again, both Pete and Verity sensed a change had taken place.

"It's going to be all right, isn't it?" Verity said breathlessly.

Pete handed her the reins and climbed down off the wagon. "It certainly is. I don't know just how, but. . .yes." He untied Sandy, mounted, and rode around to bid Verity good-bye.

"Thank you," she said, brushing a brown lock from her eyes.

He nodded and smiled. "You're quite welcome."

"Good-bye," she said, and urged Thunder and

Lightning forward, down the drive. They didn't need to be asked twice. Their stalls and suppers awaited.

"Au revoir," he corrected under his breath as Verity and the wagon disappeared behind the big McCracken barn in the distance. "We'll meet again."

Chapter 4

That evening during supper, Jacob McCracken asked Verity, "How was your trip to town? Did you remember to get my peppermints?"

"Oh, yes, Papa," his daughter said, nodding at the neat paper packet sitting on the kitchen counter.

Jacob sawed his pork chop. "And flour? You get that flour your mother needed?"

He popped a large portion of meat in his mouth and chewed rapidly, his eyes darting back and forth between the two women in his family.

Grace McCracken nodded and helped herself to applesauce. "That's funny. I could have sworn it was you that unloaded it." She winked at Verity.

"Oh, yeah. Guess I did." Jacob cleared his throat. "See anybody in town?" he asked, shaking the pepper shaker vigorously over his plate.

"Oh, you know," Verity said casually, "the usual people you see. Mr. Bernard at the mercantile, of course, and Miss Reilly at the library."

"See any Delormes?" Jacob said, and sneezed violently.

"God bless you, Papa." Verity filled her voice with concern as she racked her brain for an evasive answer.

"The Del—wha—wha—" Jacob struggled to speak, sneezed again twice, then wiped his face with his napkin. "What about Delormes? You see any of 'em?"

Verity had never lied to her Papa in her life. She dropped her fork. "Oh, dear, just a second." She ducked under the oilcloth table cover. "I think perhaps I saw Pete Delorme in town," she said from beneath the table. When she popped back up in her seat like a duck on a pond, her face was red. Verity lay the fork on the table, picked up her spoon, and began eating her applesauce. "Mmm," she said, and blinked rapidly, "everything's so delicious, Mama."

At least I didn't lie, she told herself.

Jacob opened his mouth to speak.

There was a knock at the door. "I'll answer it." Verity hurried out of the room, relieved to be away from her father's suspicious stare. *Oh, dear Lord, I hate this! Please help our family!* she prayed.

The knocking continued, growing in insistence and ferocity. Verity's hand shook as she turned the big oval brass knob and pulled the door open. "Why, Mr. Delorme, hello!" she said pleasantly.

Gerard had no corresponding greeting. "I'll thank you to fetch your father, young lady!" he snapped, and pushed past her into the dark front parlor.

Verity scurried after him and lit the gas lamp.

"Certainly," she assured him, "just a moment. He's at supper."

"I don't care if he's at the county fair! I would speak with him forthwith! Run along!" Gerard paced a circle in the room, jingling change in one of his pants pockets.

Verity left and returned quickly, with her father close behind, napkin still in hand. "What's all this about?" she heard him say as he stepped into the parlor.

With a grunt, Gerard slid the heavy pocket door closed. Just as it slammed into place, Verity heard him whisper gruffly, " 'The course of true love ne'er did run smooth,' my friend—"

True love? My friend?

Verity slipped into her seat at the big kitchen table. "Mama, that's Mr. Delorme in the parlor. Please tell me what's going on!"

Grace McCracken rolled her eyes. "I promised I wouldn't, dear, but please believe me when I tell you that there's nothing to worry—"

A tremendous roar from the parlor interrupted her. "HOWWWW DAAARE YOU, SIR!"

"Jacob?" Grace said in a small voice. She and Verity hurried to the front hallway and stood uncertainly outside the parlor door, listening, as a wild argument raged behind it.

"My goodness, Delorme, you ain't got the manners of a goat, coming into a man's own house like this!" Jacob's voice cracked as he shouted the words.

" 'How sharper than a serpent's tooth it is—' " Gerard

intoned, but Jacob interrupted.

"One more word of that Shakespeare guff, Gerry Delorme, and I'll punch you right in the nose!"

The women gasped and clung to each other.

"Oh, that's right, I'd expect violence from a clod like you!"

"Waaal, don't dish it out if ye can't take it!"

"Ignoramus! Savage! Imbecile!" Gerard's voice became higher with each word.

"Don't you go throwin' that high-falutin' lingo at me, you puffed up ol' snob," Jacob growled, "You got your education at that one-room school same as me. Everybody knows that the swill you spout come right out of that Bartlett quote book!"

There was a pause.

Grace and Verity held their breaths.

"I see that I am no longer welcome here," they heard Gerard declare in a clear, even voice. There were fumbling noises and the heavy pocket door opened, sliding back into the wall with a decisive thud. "I will take my leave now. Excuse me, please, ladies." He shouldered his way past Grace and Verity and out the front door with Jacob hard on his heels.

"You are kee-rect, Mr. Delorme, you ain't welcome here and never will be again!" Jacob shouted after the retreating Gerard. "And that goes for your entire family!"

Then he turned on his heel and marched back into the kitchen, stuffing his napkin into his collar as he walked. "Let's eat!"

"Have you forgotten what's supposed to happen next week?" Grace's voice floated up from the kitchen as Verity descended the stairs three hours later.

She cringed at the sharpness in her mother's tone and pulled the cord of her dressing gown tighter. The hall clock struck eleven times. She frowned. Mama and Papa always went up to bed at nine sharp.

Verity had excused herself from the supper table shortly after the evening's painful scene, leaving her pork chop untouched. She had performed her evening chores mechanically, then had gone up to bed early. An empty, grumbling stomach had awakened her and sent her downstairs for a glass of milk.

"Y'ain't listenin'," Jacob was saying wearily. "We got nothin' to worry about."

"We're going to need the Delormes' help with the apple harvest!"

"They'll help, they'll help, you'll see. I already told you a dozen times: We know what we're doing." Verity heard a long yawn. "Grace, we gotta get some sleep. Let's go on up to bed."

Verity slipped into the darkened parlor just before her parents mounted the staircase. "I just hope you're right, Jacob," she heard her mother say, "I surely do."

Verity slipped to her knees and laid her head on the rough horsehair of the old settee. "Dear Lord," she murmured into the worn fabric, "something terrible and strange is happening to my family. And to the Delormes."

A tear slid down her cheek and sank rapidly into the seat.

She sniffed and wiped away the others that followed with the back of her hand. "Whatever has gone on between Papa and Mr. Delorme, please send Your Holy Spirit to replace this terrible anger with peace and forgiveness. And please," she whispered as a sob rose in her chest, "show me what I should do. I feel so alone. There's nothing I can do. . ."

You can keep praying.

A still, small voice from somewhere inside her resounded. She had heard the voice before.

And you're not alone.

The image of Pete Delorme's face floated into her mind. Verity sat up. Of course! She wasn't alone. She had a prayer partner in this crisis. A nameless joy rose into her throat.

"Oh, thank You, Lord! In Jesus' name I pray, amen."

She rose and hurried to the kitchen, forming hopeful plans in her mind as she poured herself a glass of milk and sliced off a piece of Mama's good bread. Tomorrow morning, she was to go into town and meet at the school with the other teachers to prepare for the upcoming school year. Somehow, she would manage to see Pete.

Verity sighed happily as she chewed the last of the bread. God was already working this all out.

Chapter 5

The next morning, Jacob McCracken waited for Gerard Delorme at the stile until seven o'clock before giving up and returning home to begin his chores. "Hope he's okay," he mumbled. "I was afraid he'd bust a gasket last night. But it sure was a rip-snorter of a show." Jacob slapped his knee in pleasure and laughed all the way back through the elderly, gnarled trees, festooned with ripening apples.

"I'm so sorry to interrupt your work this way, Mr. Delorme," Verity said as she shook hands with Pete in the front room of the offices of Essex and Westcloth, Esquires, Attorneys at Law. "I would never disturb you if it weren't very important. This should only take a few minutes."

"No disturbance at all, Miss McCracken," said Pete gallantly. He turned to his employer, who stood smiling at him from his office door. "I've just finished my work on the Albany brief, sir." He handed the older man a thick manila folder.

Theodore Essex quickly leafed through the pages. "Well done, Pete! If this work is as good as what you did on the last one. . .well, you certainly deserve a few minutes off. Go on, buy Miss McCracken a phosphate." He winked and pulled out a large pocket watch. "It's two now. I won't expect you back till our strategy meeting at three."

Verity's eyes widened and she opened her mouth to speak, but Pete took her quickly by the elbow and steered her to the door. "Thank you, sir. I really appreciate it."

Verity descended the steps to the street in a cold silence, then stopped on the sidewalk, and turned to address Pete. "Mr. Delorme, if you think I came to your office just to. . .to. . ." She groped for a word. "Lollygag. Well, you've got another think coming!" She spun away and began walking down the sidewalk. "And I'll thank you to inform your employer that I am not thirsty and have no need of a phosphate or anything else!"

Pete hurried after her. "Ver—er, Miss McCracken, I'm terribly sorry. Mr. Essex had no business assuming anything, but he's really a nice man, when you get to know him." He circled around her, halting her progress. "I'll be sure to correct his impression when I get back to the office. But, first, please, tell me why you came. Come on, we can talk over there, in the park." He gestured toward a bench, then held up his right hand. "No phosphates involved, cross my heart."

Verity had been staring at the ground. She lifted her face to look at his and said, as the hint of a dimple played on her cheek, "Promise?"

Pete felt a surge of warmth in his face. "Didn't you see me cross my heart?" he said playfully. "A man doesn't do a d—drastic thing like this unless he m—means it." It was an old bantering line he'd used with many girls back at college, but somehow, the words took on new meaning when he spoke them before Verity's sparkling blue gaze.

Verity sighed. "All right." She proceeded briskly across the street to the park bench and sat down, waiting for him to join her.

Pete eased himself down on the bench, a good arm's length from Verity, and directed his gaze forward. "Please. Tell me," he urged, trying to ignore the gentle scent of the Yardley's lavender soap now floating on the cool autumn breeze. He wondered if Verity was warm enough in that short-fitted jacket. Quickly, he blinked away the idea of putting his arm around her shoulders and pulling her close.

Verity spoke slowly, nodding to indicate her seriousness. "It's about our fathers. . ."

By the time she had finished telling the tale of last night's horrifying scene, Pete had forgotten his reserve and was looking full into her animated face.

When a sheen of tears had formed over those remarkable eyes, he had been quick to pull a clean, monogrammed handkerchief from his pocket. He wanted to dab the moisture from her smooth, pink cheek. Instead, he handed the cloth over wordlessly and the grateful glance she gave him was worth all his forbearance.

He said, "I wondered where Father had gone last night after dinner. He wouldn't speak of it when he returned, but he looked exhausted. This is just so strange. . . ."

"I thought. . .I mean, perhaps, could we pray about this again? You know, 'Where two or three are gathered together in my name,' " she quoted with a faint smile, neatly folding the used handkerchief and depositing it in her reticule, the drawstring bag that hung from her slender wrist. It would be laundered, ironed, and returned, in accordance with etiquette.

"Matthew 18:20," said Pete. He was getting good at citing quotes, thanks to his law training. He bowed his head and began to speak in a low, gentle tone. In simple terms, he stated the problem and humbly asked God's help, then paused.

Verity spoke then, adding her agreement and thanking the Lord in advance for His divine guidance.

"In Jesus' name, amen." They said the final word together.

" 'If two of you shall agree on earth as touching anything that they shall ask, it shall be done for them by my Father which is in heaven,' " Pete said, "That's the promise that comes right before your quote."

"It does, doesn't it?"

All at once, Pete had an idea. It was so amazing, so powerful, so right, he was astounded he hadn't thought of it before. As Verity sat watching in puzzlement, a multitude of expressions rapidly passed across his broad, friendly countenance.

He's a grown-up now, Verity thought with sudden insight. *I've been seeing him as that nice, silly older boy, but he's really a full-grown man. Such a nice man, too.* A flattering blush tinted her face.

"Miss McCracken," Pete began, "Um, may I call you Verity?"

"Pete, we've called each other by our first names all our lives, up until this year," she pointed out. "Funny, isn't it? I guess it just seemed more proper, now that we've grown up." Verity found herself wondering how it would feel if she snuggled into the shelter of Pete's right arm. She would probably feel safe, and it would be nice to bring her face next to his. . .

She stiffened her back. Such thoughts were not proper.

"Verity, I just had an idea. It's a little crazy, but it might help things."

꧁꧂

At half-past seven that evening, there was a gentle tapping at the window of Gerard Delorme's first-floor study.

Gerard looked up from a volume of Shakespeare's sonnets. It was clear to anyone with eyes that he hadn't been reading. The reading glasses that had become so essential in the last few years were perched uselessly atop his shiny forehead. Gerard opened the window.

"What are you doing here?"

Jacob McCracken poked his head and shoulders through the window and leaned on the sill. "Where was ye this morning? I waited 'til I couldn't wait any more," he said in a hoarse whisper.

"I was told I was no longer welcome," Gerard whispered back coolly. He placed a firm hand on Jacob's shoulder and pushed. "Now get out of here."

Jacob's wiry frame was made up of solid muscle, tempered by hard farmwork, and he wouldn't be budged if he didn't want to be. "What are you talkin' about, Gerry? That was actin', just like you said!" He chuckled. "Boy, oh boy, we sure give 'em an earful, didn't we?"

Gerard pulled his hand back and crossed his arms. "Acting, was it? What about the names you called me? And threatening to punch me in the nose? You actually drew back your fist!"

"I had to make it sound real, didn't I? 'Sides, it seemed to me that you did your share o' name-callin', Gerry. You called me a savage!" Jacob climbed over the sill into the room, "What's wrong with you? You turn up at a fella's house, sayin' things are goin' too slow; we gotta do something dramatic. I was trying to make it good, like you said!" He closed the window carefully.

"Too good! I know the ring of truth when I hear it! You actually meant those things!"

They continued to speak in whispers.

"O' course I didn't. I was makin' it all up, just puttin' in a few details to make it sound like the real thing."

"What about the one-room school?"

"Well, it's true, ain't it? We did get the same schoolin'. You was always better with books, that's all. You know how it is—some of the kids was jealous—they said things—"

"Which you remembered all these years and saw fit to repeat in front of your wife and daughter. I don't appreciate it, Jacob!"

"Well, it warn't my bright idea in the first place, you know. You're the one come up with this Romeo and Juliet nonsense."

"It isn't nonsense; it's eminently feasible. Ingenious—"

"Well, it ain't workin', far as I can see, and I'll be glad to get shed of it."

Gerard stalked to the window and pulled it open again. The heavy curtains blew in the brisk autumn wind. "Then, by all means, take your leave."

Jacob lifted one leg over the sill. "Well, then, I will. All this stuff and nonsense was a waste of time, you ask me." He finished his cumbersome exit and turned for a final word through the window. "If you start something, Gerry Delorme, you should do it right and stick with it through to the finish. I'm shaking the dust of this place off my feet and not lookin' back."

"And I am happy to wash my hands of you, Jake McCracken. Thank goodness I finally learned your true colors. You are on your own from now on. You and your sorry excuse for a farm. Don't count on any more help from the Delorme clan."

He pulled the window closed and drew the drapes over it, leaving Jacob to trudge home, across the fields and over the stile, gradually realizing that, because of a few ill-chosen words, he might just lose the farm that had been in his family for three generations.

Chapter 6

Pete urged his horse, Sandy, forward in the autumn wind. He breathed deeply of the brisk evening air and thought about Verity. How comfortable it had been to sit on that park bench and make plans with her. How natural it seemed now to be riding to Jacob McCracken's house to ask permission to court her.

"Of course, once our fathers have patched things up, there will be no obligation on your part to maintain the charade," he had hastily assured her. "You will simply say you've changed your mind, and I will accede to your wishes."

"Oh, of course," Verity had answered, studiously straightening the cuff of her glove. "That's exactly what I'll do. . .once things are better."

"Right," Pete had said, wondering why her quick compliance gave him a sinking feeling.

"You know why, you idiot," Pete told himself aloud as he posted jauntily along the dark country road, "because she is just about the most adorable girl in the world and you wish this courtship were real. Because you. . .love Verity."

"I. . .love. . .Verity," he repeated, trying out the taste of the words. He found them delicious.

"Come on, Sandy," he said, urging the horse forward again; "we're almost there."

At the same moment, the object of Pete's affection was, herself, pacing the floor of her room and worrying. There had already been a complication in their plan and she had utterly no idea what to do about it.

"I'll prepare Mama and Papa for your arrival," she had told him during that cozy meeting on the park bench. "Right after supper, I'll sit them down and explain that you and I would like to court. There will be some resistance at first, but they'll come around, I know," she said, smiling affectionately at the thought of her fond parents. "You schedule your arrival for around eight o'clock. That should give me plenty of time."

Pete had agreed, nodding, and tilting his head in that way he had of showing he was taking in the speaker's every word. It was so nice to be taken seriously like that; to have one's opinion sought in a matter of importance. Pete's dark brown eyes, so unusual and striking in a person with blond hair, seemed to see and understand everything.

"Well," he'd said as they arose from the bench just before his three o'clock meeting, "might as well get the ball rolling. You know, Miss Reilly over at the library has had her face pressed against the window, watching us, for the last twenty minutes. No, don't look!" he said, quickly taking her elbow and turning her towards him. "Just give me one of those pretty smiles of yours, and I'll escort you back to the buggy."

It had been fun, thought Verity, smiling at her image in the bedroom mirror, to pretend to be falling in love.

And even if it were real, Pete wouldn't be a bad choice at all. He had been so gallant, helping her into the buggy. Another memory floated into her head, that of the adorable, eager way he had retrieved her hat. And strong. The way he had lifted—

The hall clock began to chime and Verity was jerked back to the urgent present.

After supper, Papa hadn't remained seated at the kitchen table, smoking his pipe as he always did. Still chewing his last bite of custard pie, he had taken a gulp of coffee and said, " 'Scuse me. Gotta go check on something. Should be gone for a bit." Then he had disappeared out the back door. Verity's chance for a family conference disappeared with him.

"Where could he be?" she murmured as the last of the eight chimes rang. "Pete will be here any minute!"

The back door slammed and Verity flew down the stairs to the kitchen.

Jacob, looking bedraggled, was back at his place at the empty table. "Got any more coffee?" he asked his wife.

"Papa, you're back," Verity announced.

"I'm back," agreed her father with a sigh. He nodded his thanks to Grace for the steaming cup she placed before him.

"But where did you go?" she blurted. "I needed to talk with you!"

"Never you mind." Jacob stirred sugar into his cup. "Nothing you need worry yourself about." He took a sip. "Where's the cream?" he asked petulantly. "Ain't we got cream in this house?"

Grace calmly placed the pitcher on the table.

Verity looked from one parent to another. Now didn't seem to be a good time to bring up the subject of courtship, but it couldn't be helped. Now or never. She straightened her spine and took a deep breath. "Mama," she began, "and Papa. I have something very important to—"

There was a brisk, cheerful rapping at the front door.

~

It had been more than an utter disaster, Pete thought morosely as he steered Sandy back down the familiar road to his father's house. It had been a defeat, a checkmate, a debacle. "A mess," Pete added to his mental list.

Things had seemed to be going well when Verity answered the front door, her eyes wide as saucers. But once she silently ushered him into the front hall, things took a steep decline into chaos.

Jacob had marched up to him. "You!" the scowling man said, sharply tapping Pete's chest with his forefinger,

"You got a lot of moxie! Are you here with your Pa's apology, lad?"

"Well, no, sir," Pete began, "I'm—"

"Then I'll have no truck with ye," said Jacob. He then spun Pete around and pushed him roughly toward the door.

"But—" Pete protested, his arms flailing.

"Papa! What are you doing?" Verity yelped.

"Jacob!" Grace added to the din, "You musn't—"

But Jacob already had, and Pete staggered down the front stairs and into the yard before he could stop himself.

The front door slammed, hard. Clearly, there was to be no earnest, dignified meeting in the front parlor between Pete and his intended father-in-law, not even a charade of one.

❧

There was a brittle silence in the McCracken kitchen. Verity and her mother were seated at the table, staring into ice-cold cups of coffee, when Jacob entered. He had spent the last half hour in the darkened parlor, pacing and thinking furiously.

The women didn't look up at Jacob when he seated himself before them. He sighed deeply and began to speak. "I better explain what's goin' on," he said.

Grace continued to avoid his gaze, but stirred her cup, tapped the spoon briskly, and placed it with great deliberation on the saucer. *Indeed you should,* her gesture seemed to say.

His wife's clear agitation disturbed him until he

caught a glimpse of Verity's melancholy expression, now turned full force on her father.

You'd think she'd already fallen for the Delorme boy, he thought, then dismissed the idea from his mind.

Grace looked at him then. Her eyebrows were high, her mouth tight. *Yes? Go on,* her face said. *We're listening.*

"This problem I've been havin' with the Delormes? Well, it just got worse."

Verity leaned forward. "What do you mean, Papa? How much worse can it get?"

Jacob avoided his wife's eyes. "The Delormes. They're not helping us with the apples this year."

Grace slid back her chair, stood, carried her coffee cup to the sink, and dumped it out. "I knew it," she said softly, still leaning against the sink, her head bowed. "I knew this would happen."

It seemed to Pete that things couldn't get any worse, but he was wrong.

Gerard called him into the study upon his arrival back at the house. "Sit down, son; I want to have a talk with you."

That's what I was hoping Jacob McCracken would say, Pete thought wryly.

It was surprisingly cold in the study. "Have you had the window open, Father?" Pete asked.

Gerard shook his head impatiently. "Never mind that. Sit down. Listen, do you remember that firm in

Saratoga that offered you a position?"

"Sure, Daugherty and Daugherty. They were my first choice. But we both decided it would better if I were closer to home."

"Well, Pierre, I think you should reconsider. As I recall, they were extremely eager to have you. I'm sure it's not too late to write them and see if the job is still open."

"Father, I've already begun work here. I like it. Mr. Essex says—"

"Ted Essex will understand, once I have a talk with him. There's just so much more opportunity in a city like Saratoga. The people you meet—"

"The people I meet won't be related to Jacob Mc-Cracken; is that what you mean? Just what is going on between the two of you, Father? Can't you see what this. . .turmoil is doing to Mother, to our family, to their family? You've been friends all your lives. Can't you find a way to patch this thing up?"

Gerard shook his head sadly. "No, son. It can't be fixed. The man has despised me all these years, and I'm only just learning of it."

"What about forgiveness? Father, can't we pray together about this?"

Gerard squirmed in his chair. "No, not now. I'm just too agitated. Maybe later." He stood and patted his son on the shoulder affectionately. "Run along and be thinking about what we discussed."

At the door, Pete turned and asked, "What about

next week? The apple harvest?"

Gerard didn't even look up from his book. "Out of the question," he said firmly, and turned a page.

Chapter 7

"Can Ben Hayward help us, Mr. McCracken?" asked Jacob's only farmhand, Fred Willard, as he helped his weary employer unhitch Lightning and Thunder from the wagon. Fred's eager expression belied his weariness. It had been a long, hard day with Jacob away in town, looking for men to pick the apples.

Jacob sighed. "Nope. Everybody's tied up with their own harvesting. I even cornered Jack Bacon in the mercantile and asked him. Offered him top dollar."

"But he's one of the Delorme hands!"

"You think I don't know that? I was desperate. I thought mebbe he and a couple of the other fellas there could spare us an hour or two, evenings, or something."

"What'd he say?" There was hope in Fred's lined, homely face as he led the two horses into their stalls.

"Couldn't. Said Delorme'd fire him if he found out—fire him for sure. I don't blame him none; he and Sally got that baby coming and all. But I'll be honest with you, Fred, I just don't know how we're gonna manage."

"Don't forget; I'm here, Papa," said his daughter, walking past, a full milk bucket in each of her hands. "Mama and I can pick apples."

"I hate to admit it, but. . ." Jacob pulled off his hat and scratched his head. "I'm 'fraid I'm gonna need ye."

"Then who'll cook for us?" Fred asked. "The thought of Mrs. McCracken's chicken pie is what keeps me goin', harvesttime."

"Mama and I will be making sandwiches the night before, Fred, so we can be free to help out in the orchard. Maybe when this is all over, Mama can make you some pie."

" 'S'all right," said Fred with a good-natured grin as he ducked down to brush down Lightning's foreleg. "I'll remind you then."

Jacob relieved his daughter of one of her buckets and helped her pour the fresh milk into the tall metal can.

"Why is he doing this, Papa?" Verity rinsed the buckets under the farmyard pump. "It's just so spiteful. Mr. Delorme knows what the apple harvest means to us."

"Hard to say. Wish I knew." Jacob repeated the trite expressions guiltily as he avoided his daughter's eye. "Can't be helped."

Grace held the back door open for them. "Hurry and wash up, Fred," she called. "It's chicken and dumplings tonight, then straight to sleep. We got a long day tomorrow."

The next morning, pink rays of dawn were moving across the sky and the rooster was crowing as Jacob, Grace, and Fred set out for the orchard in the buckboard, loaded with ladders, round bushel baskets, and a stack of rough shoulder bags.

"Wait!" called Verity from the back door. "Don't forget this!" She hefted a heavy hamper, filled with sandwiches and hard-boiled eggs. "And the water!" She pointed to the tall milk can with a curve-handled dipper hanging from it standing on the back stoop.

"Thanks, punkin," said Grace, relieving her daughter of the burden.

"I'll be along just as soon as I can," Verity assured her. "The minute I finish with the milking and the chickens. The dishes are already done."

Fred heaved the water can into the wagon. "You got a good youngun there, Missus McCracken," he said, with a wink at Verity.

The glance that Grace threw at her daughter was filled with love. "You're right, Fred, we do."

Verity stole a moment to watch them ride away. This time last year, seven Delorme hands had surrounded the wagon, full of Mama's good bacon and eggs, joking good-naturedly as they walked alongside. They always had good reason to be cheerful. They would be fully paid for the workday by Gerard Delorme and receive additional pay from Jacob McCracken.

It had been this way since long before Verity was born. The benefits of this arrangement to the Delormes were less apparent than to the McCrackens. Of course, a portion of the apple harvest was always carried directly across the stile, but it represented only a small percentage of the cost of paying the hands. Verity had always assumed that Gerard had helped with the harvest out of the goodness of his heart, but she had reason to doubt that goodness now.

A soft, reproving moo from the barn pulled Verity from her thoughts. She sighed, put on a heavy wool coat, and headed into the yard. "Coming, Matilda," she called.

Pete, feeling out of uniform in sensible overalls layered under warm wool, leaped over the stile easily and walked briskly between the orchard rows.

In the growing light of dawn, the steadily brightening redness of the apples which hung from the outside branches signaled that the time for picking was now.

After a minute, Pete began to hear the voices of Jacob and his skeleton crew of pickers, clear in the crisp air.

I figured they'd get an early start, he thought. *Good thing I did, too.*

Jacob and the others had already begun picking when Pete walked up to the wagon, pulled a sack over his shoulder, and carried a ladder to a neighboring tree.

"What d'ye think you're doin'?" Jacob snapped, and

his ladder wobbled slightly.

"I'm helping pick apples," said Pete, grasping an apple and pulling it from its branch with the gentle, twisting motion that retained the stem. He slid the apple into his shoulder bag and reached for another.

Jacob grabbed a sturdy, low-lying limb, causing half a dozen precious McIntoshes to thud to the ground. "Did your pa send ya? Is he ready to apologize?"

Pete continued to work. "Afraid not, Mr. McCracken. It's just me."

"Then I have no need of your help. Be on your way!" Trembling with rage, he struggled to descend the shaky ladder. "I'll thrash you, boy, so help me!"

Grace, who had been gathering the fallen apples for use in cider, ran quickly to the tree. Looking up at Pete, she implored, "I know you mean well, but please, go now! He'll give himself the apoplexy! Never mind the ladder; just go!"

Pete jumped down and thrust the shoulder bag into Grace's hands. "I'm sorry," he whispered. "I'll find a way to help, I promise!" Then he turned and ran back down between the rows, ducking under the low branches.

Jacob was still grumbling when Verity arrived an hour later. "How is it going?" she asked, dragging a ladder up to a tree.

"It's a-goin'," snapped Jacob.

The four worked steadily, without the cheering banter that had once been part of the fun of harvesttime.

The sun made its presence known only briefly, sliding quickly behind a slate-gray curtain of clouds. The thin, filtered light gave little warmth.

Verity's fingers, in their hand-knit woolen gloves, quickly became stiff with cold, and her wrists ached. It was also painful to realize that she was the slowest picker among them. During past harvests, her job had always been to help Mama make the gigantic hot meals that sustained the men, rolling the dough for the chicken pies, chopping the onions for the rich soup, elbow-deep in sudsy water washing the mountains of dirty dishes. It had been hard work, but it had been warm.

I've never seen a colder harvesttime, thought Verity. *In more ways than one.*

She sighed deeply, and the cold air ached as it descended to her lungs. "Dear Lord, won't you help us?" she prayed between coughs.

❧

Pete's whispered prayer echoed Verity's as he left Mr. Wessex's office. He had already apologized for being late and was prepared to throw himself into the research for an important upcoming lawsuit, but his mind still whirled from the morning's events.

Pete shook his head. Going to the orchard had been a silly, impulsive, childish idea. He should have known what was going to happen. And how would he have explained his absence to his kind employer?

As he gathered the documents he would use in his

research, Pete prayed again.

Lord, You've put me here for a purpose. Please show me a way to help, not hurt things.

He turned to his work. It was a dispute about land usage. A Mr. Gonyea was suing a Mr. Bentwell, because Bentwell wouldn't let Gonyea's goats cross his land to get to a stream. Water rights are serious business, Mr. Essex had said. This wrangle could keep the two neighbors in the courts for years.

"Don't complain," Pete reminded himself. "Disputes like these are your bread and butter." It seemed a shame, though, that the issue couldn't be resolved quickly and easily between neighbors.

Right. Neighbors like Father and Jacob McCracken? Pete snorted in disgust. Maybe the world needed lawyers, after all.

❧

To Verity, it seemed like days before Jacob climbed down his ladder and called, "All right, everybody! I reckon it's time for a rest."

Verity swayed slightly and backed slowly down to the ground. Her arms had turned to lead. The shoulder bag was filled with lead. Her whole body was made of lead.

She staggered over and slumped against the warm body of Thunder, who stood calmly as always, his breath coming out in steamy gusts. She laid her cheek against his flank and realized that her whole face was numb.

The little group gathered at the wagon, where

Jacob offered up a blessing for the meal. "And if you'd do some kinda miracle and help us get these apples to market on time, we'd really appreciate it," he said. Nobody smiled or chuckled. They had all seen the small number of apples that were picked so far.

Verity chewed gamely at the bacon sandwich her mother had given her. The bacon, once crisp and hot, had gone rubbery in the cold. She rewrapped the sandwich in its cotton napkin and peeled a hard-boiled egg. This was better, especially with the pepper and salt Mama had remembered to pack. She ate two, plus a half of a jam sandwich for dessert.

"What is it, punkin?" Mama asked. "You're shivering." She put her arms around Verity. "Let me warm you up."

Verity laid her head on her mother's shoulder. She could have fallen asleep right here, standing up in the middle of the orchard at noontime. With a supreme act of self-control, she pulled herself away. "I'm all right, Mama. Gotta get back to work."

❧

"But what does he hope to gain by not settling this case?" Pete cut into a slab of pot roast, stirred the piece around in the rich, brown gravy, and put the forkful into his mouth.

"Bentwell's strategy is to use every delaying tactic in the book, just to draw this thing out," Mr. Essex said. "He knows Dan Gonyea can't afford to spend a lot of money."

Pete swallowed. "But Bentwell can." He nodded. "I see. Last man standing wins."

"Exactly!" said Mr. Essex, spearing the last chunk of carrot on his plate. He had invited Pete to his home for lunch. "And our job is to keep that from happening."

"Are you ready for dessert, Mr. Delorme? It's hot gingerbread, right out of the oven," Mrs. Essex offered, "with applesauce on top."

"Yes, please."

A guilty thought passed through Pete's mind: *I wonder what kind of lunch Verity is having?*

He turned to Mr. Essex. "Sir, may I propose a hypothetical situation to you? Supposing there are these two old friends, who also happen to be neighbors. . . ?"

Verity felt that coming back to the house from the orchard that night seemed a little like entering the gates of Heaven. Everyone sat still at the kitchen table for a while, letting the warmth from the woodstove radiate into them before they spooned out the hot soup Mama had set to simmering that morning.

After draining the last drop from her bowl, Verity laid her head down on the table next to her soupspoon and fell asleep immediately.

"Verity, dear. . ."

She barely heard her mother through the sleepy fog as she was led upstairs to bed.

The next morning, Verity awoke with a sore throat.

"How are you today, Verity girl?" her father asked

as she came down to breakfast.

"You're flushed," her mother said, and reached to feel her forehead.

Verity ducked away and hurried to the stove, where she poured herself a cup of coffee. "I'm fine, Mama," she insisted, plastering a smile on her face. "Please don't worry about me."

She had gargled with salt water, added an extra layer of clothing, and pocketed a few of her father's peppermints in preparation for another long day of apple-picking.

And a long day it was. At the end of it, the results were again disappointing, and Verity overheard Jacob tell Grace, "We'll make it, but only if we keep on goin' like we been goin' for the whole two weeks."

Sore throat or no, Verity fully intended to keep going. That same terrible night he had thrown Pete out the door, Jacob had explained what could happen if they didn't get their apples to market. There were payments to be made—for seed, for the new plow, for the mortgage it had been necessary to take out five years ago. Default on these payments, and there would be no more McCracken farm.

"My great-grandfather came here from Scotland," Jacob said, repeating a story Verity had heard all her life, "as an indentured servant. But he worked hard and went on to become the most successful farmer in this county. I'd hate to let it come down to this. . . ."

The despair in her father's eyes had cut Verity to

the heart. She would use her last ounce of strength to see that such a thing wouldn't happen.

❧

Pete hadn't slept well. He had lain awake until three in the morning, thinking of the week's perplexing events and his new feelings for Verity. He had no illusion that she returned them with the same intensity. "But if we got to know one another better. . ."

He imagined a future with Verity by his side, and his heart lifted. He imagined a future without her, and sat bolt upright, then slid to his knees and prayed until his eyes would no longer stay open.

"Stop dwelling on this. It's not Mr. Essex's problem," Pete told himself firmly on his way to work the next morning. "I owe him a good day's work."

His employer called him into his office right away. Mr. Essex's eyes danced as he stood over his document-covered desk. "That hypothetical case you told me about yesterday? Well, I've done a little research, and there's something here I'd like to show you."

❧

Verity coughed and pulled another apple from another tree.

If I never see another apple for the rest of my life, I'll be happy, she thought. *If I never again taste cider, apple pie, apple cobbler, apple cake, and especially not applesauce. . .*

Even the name, "apple," sounded funny to her ear now. She repeated the word to herself, all the while reaching, twisting, and dropping, reaching, twisting, and dropping in weary rhythm. "Apple. Aaa-pull. Aaaaaa-pulllllll. Appleappleapple. . ." Verity giggled.

"Apple!" she shouted hoarsely. "Isn't that a funny word?" she called to her mother in the neighboring tree, then was consumed in coughing spasms.

"I guess so, punkin," her mother answered quizzically. "I never thought about it. Hey, I don't like the sound of that cough. Why don't you take a little break?"

"No need," said Verity, struggling not to cough again. "I'm fine." She slipped a peppermint in her mouth and reached for another apple.

"That's it!" Pete said, tapping the deed sharply with his forefinger.

Mr. Essex smiled. "It's here, clear as day. Jacob McCracken owns the strip of land that connects your father's pasture to the stream."

"But we've—I mean, our cows have been crossing over that land for generations."

"There may have been a right established, or there may not. . ." Mr. Essex twirled his pencil and nodded. "Still, Mr. McCracken could take this to court. It would be long and costly, like Gonyea versus Bentwell."

"But that would. . .oh, I see. . .turnabout is fair play, I suppose. This is rough business, isn't it?"

His employer shrugged. "It's why the Bible advises against lawsuits, but people don't always pay attention."

"What I don't understand is why Mr. McCracken

hasn't used this against my father."

Mr. Essex shrugged again. "Who knows?"

❦

I wonder, thought Verity, *if I'll be picking apples the rest of my life?* Her arms had slowed considerably in the last hour. Lifting them had become excruciating. Her back had begun to hurt, and she'd gotten shaky. She tried to steady herself by grabbing a thick branch, but she continued to quiver. "Papa," Verity said faintly, between coughs, "this ladder is. . .the ladder. . .it's. . ." She drooped over the branch, then her body began sliding down the ladder.

"Fred!" Jacob barked, "Verity! She's falling!"

Fred, who had been emptying his sack into a basket on the ground, sprang into action and caught Verity's limp form in his strong arms just in time. "Mr. Mc-Cracken! She's burning up!"

Immediately, Grace was there, too, feeling Verity's forehead. "She's got a fever. Quick; carry her to the wagon. We've got to get her indoors!"

❦

Fred Willard was pulling the buckboard onto the main road as Pete rode up on Sandy. Before Pete could greet him, Fred called, "Pete—Mr. Delorme—thank Heaven! You can go faster than I can! You gotta ride into town for the doctor. It's Verity. She's very sick! Get 'im back here, quick!"

With a troubled frown, Pete immediately turned Sandy around.

"Tell 'im it's fever—and a bad cough!" Fred called as Pete dug in his heels and slapped the reins.

As he rode, Pete tried to ignore the terrible sick grayness forming inside him. It was the same feeling he had had the night before, when he thought of a life without Verity.

"Fever and a cough," Fred had said. It sounded like . . .Pete closed his eyes, then opened them. No. No use thinking the worst. He would fetch the doctor, who would help Verity get well. Pete would then use the information he had learned this morning to straighten out this mess of a feud, and everything would be all right again.

That is, unless. . .

Dear Lord, he thought, *I'm so desperate. I don't know how to pray about this. . . .*

Sandy stumbled, and Pete slackened the pace slightly. He couldn't risk a fall.

"Careful, fella," Pete said to his horse. "Steady and straight into town."

Verity couldn't understand it. For days, she'd felt nothing but constant cold, but now her skin felt alive with a fiery heat.

"Here, punkin, drink this," her mother said softly as she spooned cool water gently between her lips.

Verity drank thirstily, several spoonfuls, then said, "My head. Hurts." She still hadn't opened her eyes. All at once, violent coughs wracked her body. She writhed

154

as the spasms continued, over and over. It seemed all the air was being squeezed out of her lungs. Would she ever get her breath?

All at once, with a long, squeaky intake of air, the torment was over, at least temporarily.

"My sweet baby," Grace murmured, and Verity heard tears in her mother's voice. "Poor darling." Gentle fingers stroked the hot forehead.

Verity opened her eyes slowly. "The apples," she whispered, taking shallow breaths, because she could feel another round of coughs lurking deep in her lungs.

Grace smiled. "Don't worry about that, punkin. Papa's got it all taken care of."

Verity closed her eyes, relieved. "Taken care of. . ." That meant that the Delormes had come around. Pete must have convinced his father to change his mind. "Pete," she mouthed silently. She smiled at the thought of him. She drew in a sigh and was rewarded with another violent bout of coughing.

❧

"It's whooping cough, all right," said the doctor, frowning. He shook his wet hands and accepted the clean dishcloth Grace handed him. "Pertussis. You can hear it in her chest. That whooping, squeaky sound when she tries to pull in air." He shook his head. "Possibly pneumonia, too. Serious business. Just have to let the disease run its course. Make her as comfortable as possible. Her youth is in her favor."

Everyone knew the doctor was a kindhearted man,

despite the great pains he took to conceal his kindness behind a mask of brusque frankness. "We'll know in the next few days if she's strong enough to endure the strain. Hard on the heart." He patted his shirtfront in an unconscious gesture.

"You're going to want to fill the room with steam. Keep filling up a big bowl from a kettle," he instructed, handing Grace a bottle of dark liquid, "and give her a tablespoonful of this every couple of hours, when the coughing is bad. She's not going to have much of an appetite, but try to keep her strength up. Broth, milk toast, that sort of thing."

Pete stopped the doctor on his way out. "How is she?"

"Bad." The doctor shook his head. "She's a sick young lady." He climbed into his buggy and urged his horse down the path to the main road.

Pete stood, lost in despair, watching him go.

"What're you doing here?" a sharp voice broke into the silence.

Pete continued to watch the departing buggy. "I brought the doctor," he said quietly. He turned and looked up at Jacob. "He said it's bad."

Jacob blew his nose, wiped it, and pocketed the handkerchief. "Ayah, it's bad. She's got the whoopin' cough and pneumonia."

"Oh, no."

Jacob sighed.

Pete mounted the first porch step. "May I see her?"

Jacob took a step back. "Look, Pete, I'm obliged to you for bringin' the doctor, 'n' all, but you're gonna have to leave now."

"But I—" Pete was about to say, "I love her," when Jacob interrupted him with a low snarl.

"Ain't you Delormes done enough around here? Why d'ye think my girl's lyin' up there so sick? 'Cause she's been out in the cold, workin' like a dog to help me bring in my apples, that's why! Go home and tell that to your pa! And tell him he won't have to deal with me much longer, 'cause come winter, I'm gonna lose this farm. I just hope he can sleep nights, knowin' that!"

"Mr. McCracken, if you'll just listen. I have some informa—"

Jacob stepped forward and shook his fist at Pete. "Get outa here! I don't want to ever lay eyes on a Delorme again, long as I live!"

Verity had a bad night. When she wasn't coughing, she was lying against a high bank of feather pillows, struggling for breath.

"Can't you let her lie down flat?" Jacob whispered to his wife. "Nobody can sleep that way."

"The doctor says it'll help her breathe better," Grace murmured. She ran her hand along her own collarbone. "He says there's some fluid in the lungs." She cringed and looked over at Verity. They were both remembering: Three Enfield children had died last year of the whooping cough.

Behind her closed eyes, Verity remembered, too. She thought, *I can understand how a child would die of this disease. You cough, over and over, and each time, it squeezes more air out of your lungs, until it seems like you'll never breathe again.*

She'd almost fallen asleep, but felt the ominous contractions begin once more in her chest, and she sat up. Again and again, she coughed: ten, eleven, twelve times, then drew in a long breath of blessed air with a loud wheeze. She fell back on her pillows, exhausted.

A little child would fight, she mused; *he'd struggle to breathe in the middle of the spasm. He'd wear his heart out. I just have to keep remembering, I can get my breath when the coughs die down. And they always do, eventually.*

She smiled faintly. *Pastor O'Neal would say there's a sermon in there somewhere.*

Maybe, *"They that wait upon the* LORD *shall renew their strength"?*

Patience, she thought. *I'm learning patience.* She tried to breathe in the soothing steam, but not too deeply, for fear of starting more coughs.

She wondered where Pete was, what he was doing.

Their efforts at healing the feud had been useless. *Perhaps we should have been more patient ourselves,* she thought. *But he felt as bad about it as I did.*

Dear Pete. She would have sighed, had she dared. *How kind he is. He really listens, too, which is rare. I like the fact that he's tall. And articulate. He uses words so well, but then he'd have to, if he's going to be a lawyer.*

He's strong, too. She remembered the way he had easily lifted the heavy sack of flour. *Just because he works in an office doesn't mean he can't lift. . .well, even lift me,* she thought, and a pleasurable shiver ran down her back.

Best of all, he loves the Lord. That's the most important thing.

Verity settled down more comfortably against her pillows and closed her eyes. She far preferred counting Pete Delorme's good points to counting sheep.

No matter how strong, tall, or articulate a man might be, if he doesn't love the Lord. . .

Her eyes popped open. She had remembered a dreamy conversation with her dormitory friends over hot chocolate one winter evening. "So, to sum up my perfect man," she'd said, "he's tall, strong, pious, articulate, and a bibliophile." The girls had all giggled at that last and her roommate said, "Leave it to Verity to want a bookworm!"

Dear Lord, Verity prayed, *is Pete Delorme my Perfect Man?*

Another cruel round of coughs began.

I mustn't die, she decided, as she waited for her turn to breathe.

I mustn't die, she repeated in her mind, while her chest and ribs ached from the exertion and her weakened heart beat fast against her chest. *Not yet,* she said to herself, while her air-starved lungs cringed in fear of more coughing.

Please, Lord, she prayed, *just let me live long enough to tell Pete—*

Jacob looked at his exhausted wife. "Here, let me sit with her," he said. He took the clean bowl from Grace's hands and draped a clean towel over his shoulder. "You need to get a little sleep."

Grace nodded gratefully and turned to leave. She paused at the door and beckoned him over with a crook of her finger. "I told her the apples are taken care of. What are we going to do about them?" she asked in a low voice.

"Our little girl's more important than all the apples in the world. We'll just let God and the birds take care o' the apples." Jacob kissed his wife's cheek and they exchanged weak, tear-sparkled smiles.

An hour later, as Jacob was pouring fresh steaming water in the bedside bowl, Verity said, "I heard what you said to Mama about the apples."

Jacob set the empty kettle in an enameled pan on the floor. "You what? You weren't supposed to hear that, little lady."

"I know, but Papa, what does it mean?" Verity's concern almost overcame her pain, but she was rewarded for this expenditure of energy by a renewed series of racking coughs. When she had finished and Jacob was wiping her face with a damp towel, he said, "No use lyin' to you, Verity. It doesn't look good for the farm, but once we get you well, we can make some plans. We got plenty o' choices. Uncle Roy'd be glad for my help with his lumberyard over to Elizabethtown, I know, and—"

"Papa, please promise me. . ." Verity waited a moment to summon more strength to finish her sentence. ". . .you'll forgive Mr. Delorme."

Jacob turned and deposited the towel in the enamel bowl. "We don't need to talk about that right now," he said, keeping his back turned.

Weakly, she tugged at her father's sleeve. "But we do. If I'm going to die, I don't want. . ."

Jacob spun around. "Verity!" he said, more sharply than he meant, "Don't say that!" Tears sprang into his eyes.

The smile Verity gave him was filled with love. "Papa, don't be afraid. . .to talk. . .about it." She closed her eyes and opened them again. "I'm not afraid. . . really. . ."

Jacob took her small, chapped hand in his and a sob escaped him.

"I don't want to die. . .knowing. . .you hadn't forgiven him—oh—" she moaned and grasped her chest, and more coughs shook her, over and over.

Oh, dear God! Jacob prayed as he watched the merciless coughing jerk her frame about on the bed. *Have mercy on my little girl!*

"You must," Verity insisted when at last she could rest. "You must forgive him. . .now. Pray," she insisted, pushing the word out with effort.

"I don't know if I can, Verity." Jacob's face was soaked with tears.

Verity smiled weakly. "Just be willing. . .to be willing. . . ," she whispered.

"What?"

"God will do the rest." She closed her eyes. She was waiting.

So Jacob McCracken bowed his head and prayed a distinct but unlovely prayer. "Dear Lord in Heaven," he began gruffly. "You know what's been goin' on between me and Gerry Delorme. I know it's not Your will that we're on the outs like this, but we can't seem to stop ourselves. I don't much feel like it, but I want to do things Your way, so if You don't mind, would You make it possible for me to forgive that ol'—sorry, Verity—to forgive Gerry? And all the Delormes, I guess. I ask it in Jesus' name, amen. 'Fraid that's the best I can do," he added, speaking to his daughter.

Her faint answer had the ghost of a giggle in it. "It was just. . .perfect, Papa. Perfect."

Jacob bowed his head again. "And while you're at it, Lord, would you heal my girl?" He squeezed her hand gently and Verity responded with a faint, but clear squeeze of her own.

Then, for the first time in twelve hours, Verity drifted briefly off to sleep, holding her father's hand and smiling.

❧

Jacob and Grace established a routine that week, taking turns sitting by Verity's bedside while the other slept. Fred gamely handled the other vital tasks alone, milking the cows, seeing to the chickens, and the hundred other small tasks a farm required. He steered clear of the orchard, though. When Verity got sick, they had all rushed back to the house, leaving baskets, ladders, and sacks scattered about under the trees. No need to fetch them now. The sight of that mess, and all those ripe McIntoshes, surely by now having fallen uselessly to the ground, would have broken his heart.

Chapter 8

I was wrong!" announced the doctor on the seventh day of Verity's illness. "Thank heaven, I was wrong!" He put his stethoscope back in his bag and stood up, a triumphant grin on his face. "Miss Verity, I know you don't feel like it right now, but you're getting better. The fever was over days ago and that rattle is completely gone from your chest. I must have been wrong about the pneumonia." He beamed down at her.

"Praise the Lord!" Grace gasped and clapped her hands. "Oh, my! I've gotta go wake Jacob and tell him. 'Scuse me." She scurried out the door.

The doctor continued. "This doesn't mean you can get up and dance a jig right away, though. You'll have this cough for a couple more months. It'll get better gradually, then finally go away entirely. You just need to rest, eat, smile a lot. . ."

Verity complied faintly.

"Good, but weak. You need to give it a little more

practice. Now, is there anything else I can do for you?" He bent over the bed for her response.

"Would you tell. . .Mama and Papa. . .to bring me something to read? They think I'm too weak, but I'm getting really bored." She launched into her habitual coughing.

The doctor waited patiently until she was once more settled comfortably and said, "That's an excellent sign. I'll have Miss Reilly over at the library give me some of her newest books to bring you. Good afternoon," he said to Grace at the door. "Good afternoon, Mr. McCracken," he said, addressing Jacob, who was tousle-haired and bathrobe-clad, but beaming back at the doctor.

"I never thought I'd ever say this, but I don't even care about losin' this ol' farm," Jacob told Grace when she returned from escorting the doctor to the door. "Tryin' to save it nearly lost us the most important thing we got." He hugged his wife tightly and smiled down at Verity. "Why, I feel so good right now, I'm almost ready to forgive that polecat, Gerry Delorme!"

Verity dipped her eyebrows in mock disapproval. "Papa."

He patted her blanket-covered foot. "Well, anyway, I can't seem to get up a good mad at him anymore. That's progress, wouldn't you say?"

"I guess so."

There was a loud slam and the sound of heavy boots running on the ground floor.

"What on earth?" Grace backed out of her husband's arms and looked out Verity's door. "What is it, Fred?"

Fred stood in the doorframe, breathing hard. "Sorry to break in on you folks like this—hello, Verity—but it's the Delormes—they're in the orchard—stole nigh unto all them apples!"

"What?" Jacob roared. He began untying his bathrobe. "Let me get dressed. I'll be right down."

"Papa. . . ," Verity called from the bed, "remember your prayer. . . ."

Chapter 9

Pete hefted another bushel basket over the stile to a burly Delorme farmhand. "There," he said, as perspiration flowed freely down his face, despite the chilly air. "That's the last of it for now. We'll be back in a few days to pick the rest." McIntosh apples, he knew, ripened from the outside of the tree in, making it necessary for pickers to go over the trees several times.

"You fellows go on back. I'll be along in a minute." He leaned against the fence, pulled out a bandanna, wiped his face, and looked down the even rows of apple trees.

It had been a good week's work. Close to three hundred bushels picked already. The McCracken apples had ripened early and would bring a good price at market.

Slowly, he folded the bandanna in neat squares, remembering the afternoon in the park when Verity had borrowed his handkerchief. How lovely she had been! How long had he loved her? Two weeks? All their lives? It didn't matter. All that did matter was that Verity must get well and be able to hear him tell her so.

"Delorme! Pete Delorme!"

Pete opened his eyes and smiled at the sight of Jacob McCracken as the man came walking swiftly towards him.

What is he doing? Is he going to hug me? Pete stepped forward and opened his arms.

Jacob never hesitated. Pulling back his fist as he walked, he swung and landed a ferocious blow in Pete's middle.

Pete bent double and staggered slightly. "What are—" he managed to say before Jacob landed a sharp uppercut to his jaw. He slumped slightly against a low-hanging branch and looked up in time to see Jacob's fist headed for his face again.

"Mr. McCracken! Stop it!" Fred Willard threw himself between the two men and sustained a painful bruise to his shoulder for his trouble.

"Let me at 'im, Fred!" Jacob barked, bouncing on his feet. "Thief! Rotten sneak thief! My daughter's on her deathbed and you're out here stealin' a man's—"

"Deathbed!" gasped Pete. "Oh, no! Verity!" With his arms clasped around his middle and blood trickling from a split lip, Pete staggered past Jacob and Fred and began running down the rows through the orchard, in the direction of the McCracken house.

"Let me go, Fred!" said Jacob, struggling in the strong grip of the other man's sturdy hands. "I'll teach him to steal my apples!"

None too gently, Fred pushed Jacob against the stone wall and shook his head decisively. "Nope. Not till you calm yourself down. I'm not about to let murder be done, Mr. McCracken, no matter what that boy stole!"

"But—"

"You coulda killed him. He warn't about to fight back, didn't you see that? *Fret not thyself because of evildoers,* the Good Book says. *Vengeance is mine, saith the Lord.* You know what that means, Mr. McCracken?" He shook Jacob's shoulders. "Eh? Do ye?"

"Yes." Jacob took a long, shuddering breath and slid down the side of the low wall until he was seated on the cold ground. "Thank you, Fred Willard," he said, his eyes closed. Then he covered his face with his hands. "Thank you," he repeated.

⁂

Half an hour later, Grace met the two men at the back door. "I got coffee made. You two look like you could use it."

"Pete Delorme. He was headed here. Did you see him?"

Grace turned and walked into the kitchen. "Ayah. I did."

Jacob and Fred followed her.

"Where'd he go?" Jacob walked over the kitchen window and pulled back the curtain. Night was falling. It was hard to see out. He seated himself at the table.

Grace put three cups on the table and poured coffee in each one. "He's here."

"You let him in?" Jacob's chair scraped the kitchen floor, but Grace put her hands on her husband's shoulders.

"I most certainly did. You sit yourself down, Jacob Aaron McCracken, and quit bein' a bull in a china shop. Drink your coffee. Here's the cream." She set the pitcher in front of him.

Fred watched her curiously from behind his coffee cup.

Jacob poured the cream, spilling a good deal on the table. "Where is he, then?"

"In Verity's room."

At the top of the stairs, Grace turned and put her fingers to her lips. "Shhhh."

Followed by Jacob and Fred, she tiptoed to the open door of the sickroom and looked fondly on the scene within.

Verity lay quietly against her high pile of pillows, a tender smile on her lips.

Pete was slumped on the floor beside the low bed. He had laid his head and right arm next to her pillows. His eyes were closed and a low, regular snoring emanated from his slackened mouth.

And, as if in time to the rhythmic snoring, Verity's slim fingers stroked his damp, blond head.

Jacob gasped.

Verity looked up. Her eyes widened, then softened.

"Papa," she began. Her hand continued its caress. "Pete loves me, did you know that? He loves me, and guess what else—" She reached for a nearby towel as coughs began to shake her body. "He. . .saved. . .our. . .apples!"

Chapter 10

"Father felt as bad about the quarrel as you did," Pete explained to Jacob one clear October evening a month later, "but his pride was hurt and the whole thing just seemed to mushroom."

Jacob stirred uncomfortably on the horsehair settee. He was dressed in his best Sunday suit, and the collar was a mite tight. "The important thing is, he did the right thing when it mattered most, and I'll always be grateful to him for that."

"Well...," Pete took a deep breath, "he had a little help...."

"Why, of course he did. All those hands pitched in, and you did, too. By the way, I gotta say again how sorry I am about that ruckus I kicked up—"

Jacob grimaced as Pete stroked his jaw, then replied with a wave of his hand. "It's forgotten, remember? Forgiven and forgotten. But there is something I am obligated to tell you, and since it might prove to the detriment of my father, it's rather difficult. . ." He pulled papers out of a leather case, spread them on a nearby low table and carefully explained about the access to the water. And how Gerard had changed his mind about the apple harvest as soon as Pete had reminded him of it.

The young Delorme shot a worried glance toward Jacob as he spoke. "Of course you could—and still can—give my father all sorts of legal trouble over this. But it's your right to know about it." He gathered up the papers carefully and replaced them in the case, nervously avoiding Jacob's eye.

"To tell you the truth," Jacob McCracken began, crossing his arms over his chest and twisting his face into a frown. "To tell you the truth, I already knew all about that." Jacob leaned forward. With a stifled grunt, he hauled up one ankle and placed it on his knee.

Pete's jaw dropped and he shook his head slowly from side to side. "You knew? But how long have you known?"

Jacob retied his shoe, then dropped his foot to the floor with a thump. "Pretty much all my life. Delormes been takin' their cows to that stream since back when my grandpa ran this place." He leaned back in the settee, then sat up straight again. It was not a comfortable piece of furniture.

The two men studied each other for a long moment before Pete broke the silence.

"Sir. Mr. McCracken. You are truly a remarkable man. I can understand where Verity gets her strength of character. To think that all the time you and my father were quarreling, you could have used this against us." Pete stood. "Even when faced with certain ruin, you never said a word about what a debt of kindness our family owed yours. What a true Christian gentleman you are." He extended his hand. "Mr. McCracken, may I shake your hand?"

Jacob's eyes twinkled as he returned Pete's firm handclasp. He spoke slowly, carefully. "I'm, er, grateful for the kind words, young man. Tell you the truth, in all the excitement, it's hard to say exactly what was goin' on in my mind. I'd like to be able to tell you that I was too noble to do down your pa, but—if I was to swear to it— I believe I'd have to say. . ." He gestured for Pete to resume his seat on the handsome chesterfield chair opposite him. "I'd have to say, I probably plumb forgot all about it." He spoke in an even, almost impassive tone, but his face at once screwed into a cheery grimace. Tiny chuckles began in the back of his throat, slowly at first, then increasing in rapidity until they exploded into contagious guffaws.

Jacob gave himself completely over to the laughter. He slapped his knee repeatedly. He rocked back and forth on the settee. Hot tears squirted from his eyes. His crimson face began to ache from merriment.

"Sir," Pete interjected when the laughter finally died down. "I still prefer the first explanation."

Jacob wiped his eyes with a handkerchief. "So do I, son, so do I." He wadded the handkerchief in his pocket and leaned forward. "But look here. I know you didn't ask for this meetin' just to discuss legal folderol. Mrs. McCracken and me kind of thought you had something else—I mean, someone else—on your mind." He winked and sat back, waiting.

Pete put aside his leather case and straightened his shoulders. "Sir," he said, his expression dignified, earnest, "you were both absolutely right. . ."

Grace had her ear pasted against the closed parlor door and heard the loud explosion of laughter. She smiled. Things were going well. She stepped back and made her way down the hall to the small room at the back of the house where she kept her treadle sewing machine. Time to start an inventory. Pretty soon now, she reckoned, there would be piece goods to buy and a trousseau to run up.

A half hour later, the heavy pocket door slid open and Pete and Jacob emerged, wreathed in smiles and patting one another on the back. "He asked me, Mother," Jacob told his wife, who stood before the mirror on the big hall coat tree, donning her best hat, "and I told him we said, 'yes.' "

Grace stepped forward and gently kissed Pete's cheek.

He blushed, then pulled a slim volume from his leather case. "Uh, ma'am, may I go upstairs and speak to Verity? I brought her another book."

Grace stepped back. "No, sir, you may not." She patted his arm to remove the sting from her words. "Verity has arranged a surprise and I will go up now and fetch it for you."

Pete, bewildered, stood waiting in the hall while Jacob shrugged into his coat and grinned at him. "Be patient. They've been working on this all day."

All at once, Pete heard whispering at the top of the staircase. He looked up into the pale, smiling face of Verity as she descended slowly, back straight and step firm. Her tight grip on the banister and the large frilly handkerchief tucked into her waistband were the only concessions to the residue of frailty left behind by her illness.

She reached the hall and held out her hand to Pete. "Another book?" She took it and read the spine. "Oh, good, Browning this time."

"The boy's one o' them—whatchamacallits—book lovers," said Jacob to his wife.

"Bibliophile, Papa," said Verity softly, hugging the book to her. "The word is bibliophile."

Pete said, "The dance tonight. Can you go after all? I mean, are you able to—"

Verity nodded. "I can stay at the dance until I get tired, the doctor says. I'm not quite strong enough to dance myself, so you must let me watch you."

Pete found Verity's coat on the hall tree and brought it to her. "Nosiree! I'm not going to leave your side for a minute!"

"Where'd she get that dress?" Jacob asked as he helped his wife into her coat.

"At college, Papa," said Verity after a discreet cough into her handkerchief. "I wore it to a dance." She looked down at the skirt, pale blue watered silk. "It's a little big now, though. . ."

With a quick glance at Verity's parents, Pete made bold to plant a kiss on her forehead. "It's perfect." Her brow was cool and smooth and soft. She smelled of Yardley's Lavender.

Verity, he thought, *means truth. God has given me a true companion.*

Jauntily, he offered his arm. "Miss McCracken, shall we?"

The tiny dimple in her cheek danced. "Mr. Delorme, let's."

While Jacob McCracken held the door open, the young couple went out into the cold air and climbed into the waiting buggy.

Grace grabbed her husband's sleeve. "You didn't tell them about the announcement. What are they going to think when Gerry Delorme gets up there and tells a whole barnful of people that they're engaged?"

"They're going to think their parents are smart enough to read the signs—oops, that reminds me." Jacob hurried into the kitchen and returned with a gallon jug of amber liquid.

"Cider," he told his wife, "to toast our children and the end of this. . .this. . .applesauce war!"

177

ELLEN EDWARDS KENNEDY

Ellen grew up in the Adirondack region of New York State and now lives with her husband in North Carolina. She was an award-winning advertising copywriter before retiring to become a full-time, cookie-baking mommy. Now that her two daughters are full-grown blessings to society, she writes and volunteers at the Triangle Reading Service, reading newspapers to the visually impaired. Her mystery, *Irregardless of Murder*, was recently released by St. Kitts Press.

Sunshine Harvest

by Debby Mayne

Dedicated to my husband, Wally,
and my two daughters, Alison and Lauren

Chapter 1

Florida, Late Autumn, 1892

Mama, the workers are hungry. Surely we can scrounge together something for them to eat."

"Not now, Anna," Josephine Drake replied from her lookout on the parlor's window seat. "Your father is due home with the supplies any minute. We shall feed them then."

Staring at her mother, Anna knew they shared a striking physical resemblance. She had inherited Josephine's tobacco-brown eyes. And often, when her father approached them from behind, he mistook one for the other—for both women twisted and pinned their wavy, honey-blond hair into an identical style to get it off their necks in the humid heat of Florida. They even wore the same petite size and frequently exchanged dresses. However, Anna's similarities to her mother went no further than these superficial traits. Her personality reflected her father in most regards. In stark contrast to Josephine's perpetual indecisiveness, Anna held a strong opinion about almost everything.

A determined Anna turned and headed for the kitchen. Since their orange groves had reached full production, the harvest required week after week of long, grueling days in order to get the fruit ready for shipment. Now, with the addition of a grapefruit harvest, the days seemed to never end. The men who worked the fields were tired and hungry. She had to feed them something. But what? After three days of feeding entire families of hungry laborers, very little food remained in the kitchen pantry.

Closing her eyes, Anna silently pleaded with God, asking Him to stretch what little food they had left. *Lord, You have been good to us. Please take care of these hardworking people.*

Their family had not attended church in months. Years. Would the Lord bother to listen to Anna's prayers?

No miracles yet, she thought as she opened her eyes to find the pantry's flour bin still nearly empty. And what could have detained her father? He was hours late coming from town with the items her mother had asked him to bring.

She returned to the parlor and, sinking onto the divan, studied her weary mother once more. Josephine's translucent skin and hollow, sunken eyes reflected the laborious tasks their family had undertaken the past few years—adding acre upon acre of new citrus groves, then harvesting their first crop of grapefruit. While other farmers scoffed at the idea of marketing the sour fruit, Anna's father planted the trees anyway, at the advice of his connections in the Orient. The risk paid off. Their entire crop of grapefruit had sold long before harvest. Still, while the business decision proved a good one, Anna suspected they were not quite ready to handle this much produce.

❦

The morning wore on into late afternoon. Anna and her mother deserted their watch at the parlor window and set about tending to household chores. Suddenly, several loud knocks sounded at the Drakes' front door. Josephine flashed a glance of helplessness toward Anna. What if one of the workers had come to demand food? What would she tell them?

Anna wiped her hands on her apron as she headed for the door. Sucking in a deep breath, she then exhaled the air with a whoosh through her clinched teeth. *We mustn't keep putting these people off. They are hungry, and they deserve a decent meal for all their hard work.* Still, she dreaded an encounter with a protesting worker.

She tentatively opened the door just a crack. To her surprise, the person on the stoop was not one of their workers, but rather a tall, slim, dark-haired man in a suit. Someone from town. Obviously a businessman.

She remembered seeing him before, but only once or twice; and she wasn't sure of his name.

He took off his hat and nodded, a grim expression on his face. "I have some news, Miss Drake. I need to speak with both you and your mother."

She took a step back and eyed him suspiciously. "I don't believe we've met, sir." She wasn't about to let a stranger into the house without at least knowing his name.

"Daniel Hopkins, ma'am." His solemn expression remained unchanged.

"J—just a minute, Mr. Hopkins," Anna replied, gently closing the door and leaving the man on the stoop. She scurried down the hall to the kitchen to find her mother. "Mama, do you know a Mr. Daniel Hopkins?"

Slowly, Josephine nodded. "He's one of the businessmen who sits on the Orlando city council. Is that who's at the door?"

"Yes. He wants to come in. He has news he wants to share with the both of us."

"Then, by all means, let him in," Josephine said, patting at her humidity-curled hair. "But we can't feed him until your father returns with the goods." Anna's mother rarely let anyone leave their home without feeding them something first.

Anna went back to the door and opened it wide. "Come in, Mr. Hopkins. I'm sorry I didn't know to let you in, but—"

He offered a forced grin as he stepped forward.

"That's quite all right, Miss Drake. You can't be too careful these days. I understand."

Anna's mother had made her way back to the parlor and now stood in a prim and proper pose. She offered the best seat in the room to their guest, who took it with hesitation. As Anna drew up a straight-backed chair, she sensed a definite tension in the air. Something was wrong.

"How nice of you to pay us a visit, Mr. Hopkins," Josephine prattled. "I'd love to offer you something to eat, but I'm afraid my husband has yet to return from town with a fresh supply of groceries."

His expression changed to a look of panic. "Yes, I know," he replied, diverting his gaze and shifting in his seat. "That's what I've come to see you about, Mrs. Drake. Your husband."

Instantly, Anna knew something had happened to her father. *Oh, no,* she pleaded in silent, furtive prayer as her heart began to pound. *Please, Lord. Not Daddy.*

"Does this visit have something to do with my father?" Anna asked, a note of apprehension in her voice. "Have you seen him?"

Mr. Hopkins slowly nodded. "Yes, your father. . ." His voice trailed to silence and he looked nervously back and forth between Josephine and Anna, then around the room at the pictures on the wall. When his gaze settled upon Anna once more, he wordlessly reinforced her fears.

Her throat constricted as she rose to stand in front

of Mr. Hopkins, urging him to finish his response. "What news do you have concerning my father, sir?"

"After Mr. Drake left my shop, he went to see the mayor. I remembered something I'd forgotten to tell him, so I ran over to city hall. There, I discovered that he'd died unexpectedly while talking with the mayor at city hall." His tragically awkward announcement made, he shifted his eyes to look at the floor in front of his feet.

A creeping blackness threatened to overtake Anna, so she gulped several quick short breaths in an attempt to remain standing. Only the sight of her mother, who had already fainted and collapsed in a limp heap on the floor, kept Anna on her feet.

Without a moment's hesitation, Anna raced to Josephine, scooping her mother into her arms, cradling her like a baby. "Oh, Mama, whatever shall we do?"

Anna's thoughts spun with a thousand different denials. Surely, this Mr. Hopkins had confused her father with someone else. Daddy was much too young, too strong, to die.

Yes, she reasoned with panic. *This is just an unpleasant incident that will amount to nothing more than a tragic case of mistaken identity.*

"You must be mistaken, Mr. Hopkins," Anna said as she straightened to face him. "My father is a very healthy man. I'm sure he'll arrive home any minute."

"I am sorry, Miss Drake," he said. The sympathetic look never left his eyes. Anna stared blankly through the man. Despite the stabbing realization that Mr.

Hopkins spoke the truth, Anna's heart clung to a shard of hope. She fell to her knees and, holding her mother once again, Anna's lips moved ever so slightly in muttered prayer.

"Lord, you wouldn't take Daddy when we need him so!" In that brief moment, her faith faltered and in agony she quietly cried, "Lord, how could You do this to us?" She was unable to control the tears, now that she had given in and accepted the reality of her father's death.

Mr. Hopkins stood and crossed the room, pausing beside Anna and Josephine. "Is there any way I can help?"

A quick burst of anger replaced Anna's pain and her gruff response surprised even her. "Here's something you can do to help, Mr. Hopkins. You can go out there and tell those hungry laborers that we have nothing to feed them and that their employer has just died, leaving us without the means to provide for them."

He stared down at Anna. "I'm terribly sorry, Miss Drake. Really. I want to help."

A look of sorrow filled his eyes, and Anna sensed that he truly did care. However, she couldn't concern herself with him now. After all, her father had just died, and her mother lay unconscious on the floor. She now faced, alone, the monumental task of caring for an army of citrus pickers. All the fruit had been sold, yet no money would come in until the goods were harvested, inspected, and delivered. Meanwhile, these people and their families must be fed.

Once Josephine stirred to consciousness again, Anna released her mother and stood. She must feed the workers. But what?

Mr. Hopkins gently touched her arm and repeated his previous question. "Miss Drake, how might I help you?"

She buried her face in her hands and sighed deeply while pondering her response. "Well, sir," Anna said as she lifted her head to meet his gaze, "I appreciate the offer, but I doubt very seriously that you can help. The fact of the matter is, my father went into town to pick up some supplies and food for my mother so we could feed our workers. He was depending on the generosity of the shopkeepers to issue credit until the crops are delivered and paid for. Now we've no food. No money. No credit. Nothing."

Josephine moaned, and Anna knelt down beside her mother. Mr. Hopkins reached down and touched both women with the tips of his fingers. "I'll do what I can," he stated firmly. Then, after a moment's hesitation, he turned and walked out the front door.

Mr. Hopkins had no sooner left the house than Anna began to sob, her body heaving in agonizing wails. Consumed in her mourning, she lost all track of time. When Anna had exhausted her tears at last, she propped herself against the nearby love seat.

"Mama? Can you hear me?"

Josephine, her open eyes appearing unseeing and vacant, still lay crumpled on the floor. "James. James.

James," she chanted softly, hypnotized by grief.

The sight of her bereaved mother filled Anna with renewed pain and fear and she called out again, "Mama?"

Josephine slowly turned and faced her daughter. Her anguished expression tore at Anna's heart. "I don't know what to do, Anna," Josephine said with a shaky voice. "Your father took care of everything. Now, I'm lost."

Anna, hiccuping softly from the aftereffects of her crying spell, leaned over to pat and comfort her frightened mother. She was frightened, too. But she could see that if someone didn't take control very soon, Josephine might wind up flat out on the floor again.

"I'll manage things now, Mama. Don't worry."

Even as the promise left her lips, she wondered just how she would accomplish such a feat. A spiraling sense of despair settled on Anna's spirit and, as naturally as breathing, her thoughts became silent prayers. *Oh, Lord. Help. Please, help. Show me what to do.*

Yet, at the time she needed most to cling to her faith, again pricks of doubt assailed her, and she could no longer contain her swelling ire. With a glance upward, she prayed, *How could You let my Daddy die? How could You do this to us? Are You punishing us?*

Suddenly, a surge of self-reliance pushed Anna to her feet. All this grief and sorrow wouldn't take care of the problems at hand. It was time to act. Something must be done to feed the workers, and she wasn't even certain that the Lord would help her now. Anna marched into the kitchen and dumped the last of the flour from the sack into their largest bowl. Then, she added every feasible pantry ingredient in an effort to make the food stretch. Even so, she produced only two baskets of pitifully small biscuits and some fried lard.

Tomorrow, she would have to go into town herself and see what she could do. Maybe someone there would extend her credit. She had no choice but to somehow convince them.

The screen door slammed behind her as she carried her meager meal offerings toward the cluster of backyard tables. While she placed the baskets on the tables, the sound of horses' hooves caught her attention. Anna turned toward the road to see a half-dozen riders approaching, Mr. Hopkins in the lead. Huge saddlebags draped the neck of each horse.

Mr. Hopkins motioned for the men to dismount as soon as they reached the yard, and they paused just long enough to pull sacks and baskets from their bulging saddlebags before approaching her.

"W—what?" she sputtered, confusion etching her voice. "What's all this?"

Mr. Hopkins set his sacks down on the table first, then turned to face her. "I know this isn't much, Miss Drake, but I told some men from the church about your plight, and they wanted to do something."

Anna watched in amazement as the men continued to pull food from the sacks, her heart pounding harder with each emptied bag. *How did they manage to gather all this food so fast?*

"God is good, Miss Drake. He won't forsake you in time of need."

As her throat clogged with emotion, she half-whispered her raspy response. "Then why did He let my father die?"

Chapter 2

Daniel studied Anna Drake for a long moment. Her eyes were still swollen from crying, yet she had managed to scrape the bottom of the barrel to provide for her workers. She showed stubborn determination. He admired her for that. And he suspected that her caustic comments flowed from her fresh grief and sorrow, not from a hardened heart. At least that's what he hoped.

"Miss Drake," he said softly as he came toward her, "the Lord will take care of you and your people. He doesn't always make His plan obvious to us, so we have to learn to trust Him."

Anna licked her lips and glanced nervously toward the cluster of men who had followed Daniel to her farm. They were already spreading the baskets of food on the tables.

"I'd like for you to accept this offer, Miss Drake," Daniel gently urged. "No strings attached. However, once you get back on your feet, we'd love to have you join us at church."

"What do you care if we set foot in church?" she asked with cynicism etching her voice.

"As a Christian and a part-time lay pastor, it is my hope to be able to minister to more than your physical needs. We are here to help you find the answer to your spiritual needs as well." His gaze remained steady as he spoke. He could tell Anna was confused. Daniel was firm in his conviction, yet he felt tenderness when he looked at her.

"Miss Drake, your father and I often spoke about spiritual matters. Over the course of our acquaintance, I watched his spirit slowly soften. This morning, when we met at my store, he told me that he had recently recommitted his life to the Lord."

"Why didn't we know anything about this?" Anna asked skeptically.

Daniel shrugged and shook his head. "I'm not sure, but I do know that he did intend to share his newfound faith with you and your mother. He mentioned that he planned to bring you and your mother to church with him on Sunday."

She narrowed her gaze, then laughed in a way that didn't become her. "Now I understand. You're only saying this because my father is now unable to refute your statements. You must desperately want to add to your church roster."

Daniel was flabbergasted. "Our intentions are pure, Miss Drake, and I speak the truth, I can assure you.

Regardless of whether or not you ever attend our church, this food is yours."

He watched as she made a decision. Obviously, Anna Drake felt as though she'd been placed between a rock and a hard spot, forced to accept something from someone else.

"Okay, Mr. Hopkins, I'll accept this food, only because the workers are hungry. But tomorrow, I'll go into town first thing. This will be the last time the Drake family will ever need to accept your charity."

"This isn't a case of charity, Miss Drake," he explained as tenderly as he could. "We're Christ's children who choose to follow in His footsteps. Whatever decisions you make about attending our church are completely between you and the Lord." He hesitated for a moment before tipping his hat. "G'day, Miss Drake. We'll pray for you and your mother." Daniel's gaze was fixed on Anna, and he felt a tug at his heart. He had an overwhelming urge to protect her from future harm. "Please drop by my dry goods shop next time you come to town."

Anna stood and watched the men mount their horses. The pain lingered in her chest, but she knew she'd been hard on this fellow who obviously wanted to help. They'd only gone a few yards when she hollered, "Mr. Hopkins!"

He turned and faced her, while motioning for the other men to stop. "Yes, Miss Drake?"

She forced a smile as the tears threatened to flow again. "Thank you for all this food. I apologize for being so harsh."

He smiled back at her in a very compassionate and tender manner. "I understand. I have experienced great loss in my past, and if it weren't for the Lord and His mercy, I don't know where I'd be today." Then, he turned and rode away with his men.

Anna could only stand there and watch him leave. With the news of her father's death fresh on her mind, her mother back in the house lying in bed, and the workers still not aware of her father's death, she wasn't sure what to do next.

There was more food laid out than normal, something that would definitely raise some questions. She knew that it would be a risk to inform the workers of her father's death right now because they would fear not being paid. But Anna was determined to continue conducting business as usual, in spite of her lack of experience. She simply must learn the business—and not waste any time in doing so.

Before long the workers began to move toward the yard, where they would typically find a modest layout of food. Anna watched their eyes widen with amazement as they each drew closer to the tables.

"Go ahead and eat all you want. Whatever is left, take home for your families." As she spoke, Anna waged an internal debate. Should she wait until tomorrow to break the news about her father's death? By then, she should have a better idea of what the bankers would do for her. However, they deserved to know as soon as possible. And the last thing she needed was for them to find out from someone else.

She stood and watched as the people piled their plates high with food. They had worked hard, and they were hungry.

Once they were all seated, Anna stood on one of the empty tables and got their attention by waving her arms. As she told them the news, they all dropped their forks, one by one, and started praying. She overheard one man praying that his family wouldn't starve to death because he couldn't find another job. A husband-wife team of hired hands had their arms around each other, mumbling a prayer of thanks for the food they had to eat today. "And Lord," she heard the wife say very clearly, "please take care of Mrs. Drake and Anna."

Anna's stomach knotted. Why did these people think that prayer would help after what had happened? Obviously, their trust in the Lord hadn't budged. Yet her own faith had been shaken by today's horrible turn of events. Then again, Anna's faith had never been too strong. Not since those long-ago days when her family had come face-to-face with hypocrisy.

When Anna was a young girl, the members of their old church had shunned them after her father lost almost everything he owned in a bad business deal. Soon after, he had learned that land near Orlando was being sold for a song, and he wanted to jump at the opportunity to invest. But the church folks, including those they had considered friends, laughed and sneered, telling them that they were only looking for a pot of gold at the end of the rainbow.

One evening during those dark times, Anna overheard her parents debating what they should do. Should they listen to their mocking advisors, who insisted that they knew the Lord's will in this matter? Or should they follow their instincts and pursue the Orlando deal? Did they really want to heed the counsel of hypocrites?

Anna had lain in her bed unable to sleep as, in the other room, her father and mother bitterly recounted other times that the church folk had acted less than Christian. Their final decision to ignore the advice of these so-called friends came when Josephine Drake reminded her husband of the time that one of their field hands was in dire need of medical care. The town doctor, who just happened to be a member of their church, had turned his back on their pleas for help. No one from the church seemed to want to be bothered with someone they considered beneath them, and the man had died, leaving behind a widow and two small children. As her mother's voice carried through the thin walls, little Anna recalled the looks of anguish on the faces of the deceased man's family. Until that moment, she hadn't known the real reasons behind the worker's death.

On that long-ago night, not only did Anna lose confidence in the people who claimed to be "Christian;" her faith in the God they followed faltered as well.

No. Anna couldn't count on the aid of church folks now. She wasn't even certain she could depend on God. Her bitter memories fueled her resolve to handle this crisis on her own.

Standing back up on that table, she got the workers' attention again, this time by clapping her hands. "All business will continue tomorrow," she said. "This farm will go on, no matter what. I assure you that I will do whatever it takes to grow oranges and grapefruit, and then take them to market, just as my father always has."

A man close to where she was standing stood up and cleared his throat. "Miss Anna, I beg your pardon, but it concerns many of us that you've never run a grove before."

Anna understood their concerns. "Maybe I haven't, but I can certainly learn. If you will keep working for me, I promise to do everything in my power to maintain the same pay as before. If you choose not to, I understand. However, once the workday begins tomorrow, I'll reward those of you who remain with me."

She got down off the table and left the group to discuss among themselves what they were going to do. It frightened her to think that the whole lot of them might walk away and leave her stranded with acres and acres of oranges and grapefruit in need of harvest. But what could she do other than what she'd already done?

⁓

Anna brought some food in to her mother, knowing

she wouldn't be able to eat. The news was too new, the pain too fresh. But she had to at least try, now that she was in charge.

"What did the workers say when you told them?" Josephine asked as she tipped the cup of tea to her lips.

Anna forced herself to smile, in spite of her worry. No need to concern her mother until she knew something for sure. Tomorrow she'd have a better idea of whether or not they'd even have workers.

"They're very sad, of course," Anna said slowly. "But when I told them that tomorrow there'd be business as usual, they were relieved." She left out her feelings of anger that had taken a turn to fear of the Lord. What would He do to them next?

Josephine narrowed her eyes and studied Anna's face. Anna didn't like that kind of scrutiny, knowing that she wouldn't hold up like this for long. "They said that?"

"Well," Anna replied, unable to lie. "Not in so many words."

"Exactly what did they say?" Josephine asked.

Anna swallowed hard. She didn't want to worry her mother any more than she already was, but she couldn't lie, either. Looking down, she said, "Most of them just started praying for their families. We'll have to wait until tomorrow to know what they're going to do."

"I see," Josephine said as she looked into her cup. "Did you manage to scrape up enough food to feed them?" She glanced over at the plate of food Anna had brought up as if seeing it for the first time. "Oh, my." Her hand went to her mouth, her eyes huge from wonder.

"Mr. Hopkins and some men from his church brought food for the workers," Anna said in a soft voice.

Josephine continued staring at the plate for a moment before looking back over at Anna. "I wonder how long they'll keep this up."

"They won't," Anna replied.

With her eyebrows raised, Josephine tilted her head to one side. "And why not, may I ask?"

Anna squared her shoulders and inhaled through her nostrils, then let it out slowly as she fought hard to keep from lashing out at her mother. Josephine might be willing to accept charity, but she wasn't. When she was certain she could speak without anger in her voice, she said, "Because I told them we will not accept charity from anyone."

"Anna, these people are just doing what the good Lord wants them to." She sniffled, then added, "Or at least what they think the Lord would want them to do."

"You don't really believe that, do you?" Anna said.

"I—I'm not sure," Josephine said as she glanced away. Anna could tell she really didn't. Neither of them did.

Anna was sitting here with a citrus grove to run. She knew she must rely on her own strength rather than someone else's. After all, who did she know that could meet their needs?

"Mama," Anna said after several long moments of silence.

"Yes, Anna?" Josephine whispered. Her face was still pale, and her eyes were sunken above hollowed-out cheeks.

"What will we do about burying Daddy?"

Josephine's face whitened even more. She sank farther beneath the blanket and closed her eyes. "I have no earthly idea."

Anna reached out and smoothed her mother's hair from her forehead. "Don't worry, then, Mama; I'll take care of everything."

She'd said it, and she'd meant it. *From now on,* she thought, *I'll take care of everything—the funeral, the farm, and Mama.*

The sun had barely gone down, and there were still traces of light as Anna headed downstairs to the kitchen. She'd left the plate of food in her mother's room, knowing that it probably wouldn't be touched. Her heart was heavy, but she couldn't give in to the weakness of emotion. She had too much to do.

At first, when she heard the knock, she didn't realize what it was. The wind had been blowing, so she assumed that it was nothing more than the wind blowing a tree branch against the side of the porch. But the second time she heard it, she knew someone was at their door.

Anna paused for a moment, unsure of whether she should answer it. She didn't feel like taking callers now, but it might be important. So, she turned back toward the front of the house.

The instant she opened the front door, she regretted her decision. It was Mr. Hopkins.

"Yes, Mr. Hopkins? Did you forget something from your earlier visit?" she asked as coolly as she could without being rude. After all, he had been kind enough to gather food for her. She'd have to remember to find a way to pay him back for his generosity.

He smiled and removed his hat. "I began to think about your plight, Miss Drake—"

"You don't have to think about my plight, Mr. Hopkins," she interrupted. "We're perfectly fine." Anna had to look away from Daniel's soft, caring gaze. She couldn't allow herself to be concerned with this man who was still in God's good graces.

He stood there and studied her while she felt an unfamiliar fluttering in her abdomen. "I'm sorry, but I beg to differ. No one would be fine after hearing such sad and tragic news. I'm here to listen to you."

"I have nothing to say," she snipped.

"Please, may I come in?"

"Persistent, aren't you?" she asked as she backed away from the door to make room for him.

He chuckled softly. "I suppose that's a nice way of putting it."

"Look, Mr. Hopkins, I appreciate all you've done. I'll even go to your church once or twice to show my appreciation. But please don't feel that you have to take us on as the poor widow and daughter left behind."

"That's not how I feel, Miss Drake," he said. "And

please call me Daniel."

"I prefer to address you as Mr. Hopkins." Her voice was beginning to crack. She cleared her throat.

"Suit yourself," he said. "But may I call you Anna?"

She shrugged, not taking her eyes off him for a moment. While she felt that she could trust him to tell her the truth, she still wondered why he kept coming around. She'd absolved him of all responsibility, and just because he'd been the one sent to break the awful news that very day, he didn't have to feel it was his obligation to take care of her.

"You may call me anything you like," she finally said.

"I'd like to help with the funeral preparations if you don't mind." His voice was solid and steady, something she needed just then. "Mr. Fletcher, the undertaker, needs to know what arrangements have been made for the body, and I figured that you probably haven't had time to really consider the matter in detail. We have a small cemetery behind the church, or if you'd prefer we can bury your father on your property."

"I hadn't really thought about it," she said.

"Let me know, and I'll take care of everything."

Slowly, Anna nodded. "I'll do that. Thank you, Mr. Hopkins."

For an instant, he looked hurt, then he smiled and nodded. "The people of the congregation have offered to bring food for your workers for the next several days, until you can make other arrangements for them."

"Other arrangements?" Anna asked.

He nodded. "Surely you don't plan to continue harvesting all this fruit. After all, your father was the businessman. No one expects you—"

Anna stood up and nodded toward the door, cutting him off. "Thank you, Mr. Hopkins, but I will feed my own workers. I plan to do quite a few things that no one expects of me. I will continue harvesting the fruit, and I will take over my father's business. I thought I already made myself clear this afternoon."

He stood up and took a couple of steps toward the door. "I see." He turned around and faced her, catching her off guard, making her heart leap. With his blue-green eyes leveled on her, she felt stiff and frozen in place. "So you're telling me that you'll tackle everything all by yourself, no help from a soul other than the workers you have in place, harvesting the crops."

"That's exactly what I'm saying, Mr. Hopkins. I'm glad we've finally come to this understanding."

Mr. Hopkins tilted his head toward her but continued looking at her from beneath hooded eyes, making her dizzy with an unfamiliar emotion. She wanted to hate him, but she couldn't; his voice was too soft and filled with compassion. "I may leave you alone, but I will not quit praying for you." Then he turned on his heel and walked out the door, never once looking back.

Anna stood there staring after him, wondering what good his prayers would do if she didn't acknowledge them. She'd given up praying this very morning, knowing that if God was willing to take her father at a time like this, she must not be in His favor anyway, so why bother?

As she thought about her loss and all that lay ahead for her, Anna leaned against the wall and slowly slid to the floor. Her body began to shake with sobs, her heart feeling like it had been shattered into a million pieces. She had loved her father, despite his bitter spirit following his financial setbacks. Even after he had recovered financially, his bitterness remained. It was only lately that Anna had begun to see a softer side of her father. Now he was gone.

She must have fallen asleep on the floor in the hallway because a stream of light coming in through the window awakened her. Her eyes fluttered from the brightness of a blazing sun.

Anna stood and looked outside for her father before she shuddered with a jolt of remembrance of yesterday's tragedy. She wanted to think this was all a bad dream, but she knew it was reality. And now she had to face it. There was so much to tend to; she felt as though she was swirling in a whirlwind that would never end.

As tempting as it was, Anna simply would not ask for help from anyone, especially Mr. Hopkins. The last thing she needed was to be indebted to a do-gooder who wanted to pound his Bible in her face.

Anna hadn't been awake more than five minutes before she heard her mother call from upstairs. "Anna, come quickly. I need you."

"Coming, Mama," she called in a weak voice. She had to find the strength to stand up to what she had to face this day and each day after. There was so much to be done; she couldn't allow herself to be weak.

"Anna," Josephine said when Anna arrived at her door. "Please be a dear and fetch me some tea."

"Yes, Mama," Anna said. "But I have to run into town this morning, so I want you to try to get up and move around a little bit. At least get dressed and find a comfortable spot in the parlor, just in case someone comes to the door."

"Who would come here in the middle of the week?" Josephine asked.

"Since Daddy died, folks seem to be appearing at our door with regularity," Anna replied, envisioning the form of Daniel Hopkins as he stood on their porch. She shook her head to dispel the image and her thoughts returned to the matters at hand.

"Mama, you must help me if I am to have any hope of doing what needs to be done today. Let me get your tea, then I'll be right up to help you dress."

Anna rushed around in preparation for her trip to town. There was no time to waste. She wasn't sure if the workers had all arrived, but she knew some had. She'd have to get an accurate count this evening when they all came back to the yard for supper.

Typically, when she went into town, she rode in the carriage. But she didn't have time today to hitch the horses, so she simply saddled a horse. She would somehow manage to fit the day's food for her field hands in the saddlebags.

Fortunately, the weather was nice, so she didn't have to worry about that. The brisk air felt good on her cheeks as the horse trotted to town. Hopefully, she wouldn't be met with too much opposition from the grocer, who'd been extending credit to her father ever since he'd added grapefruit groves. People in town were excited about the new crop, so she'd use that to her advantage.

The grocer was more than happy to offer a week's worth of credit. "But, unfortunately, I can't do more. I have to pay for these items when they arrive, and if I go much longer than a week, I can't stay in business."

She nodded as she sighed. "I understand. I'll have your money to you within a week." She picked up a few items and left, feeling dejected. She had no idea how she'd make good on this promise.

Then, Anna went to the next place on her list, the bank. She was greeted with a warm smile. Maybe, just maybe, she'd get what she needed here. But by the time she left, she knew that there wasn't much hope for her to get what she needed in order to keep the groves. Mr. Blankenship, the banker her father had trusted for years, had told her in so many words that, without her father there, she might want to consider selling the farm and moving herself and her mother into a house in town.

"We have some mighty fine places here that I'm sure will more than accommodate you and Mrs. Drake," he'd said.

"That's not what I plan to do," she'd stubbornly argued. "I want to continue running the business my father started."

Mr. Blankenship had dropped the pretense of the smile and leaned forward to face her, his hands folded on top of his desk. "And exactly how do you plan to carry on, Miss Drake?"

She'd inhaled through her nose and let it out in a whoosh through pursed lips. "Obviously not with your help."

The banker had stood up and walked toward the door. "I'm sorry, Miss Drake, but this is business. I'm sure you'll understand someday."

"I understand now," she'd said in a huff as she breezed past him and didn't turn back.

Nothing had gone right. What was she to do, now that there didn't seem to be an ounce of hope?

"Miss Drake!" a voice said from behind. "Anna, please wait."

She spun around and found herself face-to-face with Daniel Hopkins. In spite of how she'd felt about him the day before, she smiled. For some reason, he didn't seem so bad today. "How do you do, Mr. Hopkins?"

Chapter 3

He looked at her as though he didn't believe his eyes. Anna watched him as he blinked back the disbelief she'd initially seen on his face.

It took him a few seconds to regain his composure. "Miss Drake. Anna," he corrected himself. "How are you today?"

Anna shook her head. "At the moment, I'm not quite sure."

"I understand," he replied. "You had so much to deal with yesterday, I'm surprised to see you out and about today."

"I didn't exactly have a choice, Mr. Hopkins," Anna retorted, her voice dropping. No matter how hard she'd tried, she hadn't managed to convince anyone she could run her father's business.

"Is there anything I can do to help?" he asked with concern.

She started to shake her head, but she stopped. "Well, maybe."

"Would you care to discuss this here or in private?"

Anna thought for a moment. She wasn't up to talking about such matters in the middle of downtown Orlando, not with all the people milling about. Besides, she still needed to pay a call on the undertaker to discuss funeral arrangements. "Would you care to come for dinner this evening, Mr. Hopkins? Perhaps we can discuss it then."

He glanced down at the meager sacks of food in her hands and slowly shook his head. "I wouldn't want to come for dinner. I'm not one to do something so ghastly as eat all the food intended for farmhands."

"Nonsense," Anna said as she shifted the sack to her other hand and put it behind her skirt. "There's plenty."

Mr. Hopkins continued to scrutinize the situation before he finally nodded. "Yes, then, I'll be there."

"Good," she said as she tilted her head back jauntily. "I'll expect you at five-thirty."

The instant he walked away, Anna glanced down in the bag she still held in her hand. He was right. She didn't even have enough food for the farmhands, let alone for someone like him. What would she do?

Pulling her drawstring purse open, she glanced inside to see how much money she still had. Three dollars. That used to seem like quite a bit of money to her, but not now. It wouldn't last long if things didn't change around here very quickly. She was afraid she might have to take Mr. Blankenship's suggestion and sell the groves to the highest bidder.

Moving into town wouldn't be so bad, she thought. At least she wouldn't have to worry about feeding the workers. There were other things she remembered her father fretting over. Drought, for one. There were seasons when he watched the sky and prayed for rain. When it didn't come, he always blamed God. When it did, he spoke of how good of a farmer he was. Another thing he'd had to worry about was frost. She remembered her father saying, "A cool snap is good because it sweetens the fruit, but a deep freeze is bad. One long freeze could put us out of business for good."

Yes, moving into town just might be the answer. But she didn't want to admit defeat. Not yet, anyway. She still had some fight left in her. Anna Drake was born on a farm, and she was determined to keep it as long as she humanly could, despite what all the naysayers in town thought. Just because she was a young woman, barely an adult, didn't mean she wasn't smart enough or didn't have what it took to run the groves and have a successful business.

But each person she spoke with, each possible lender who could keep her from losing her battle, brought her closer to being forced to move. Her father wasn't even buried yet, and here she was about to lose everything. Anna and Josephine didn't even have the luxury of mourning his passing.

Actually, her mother didn't seem to care what happened. She'd always been one to drift along, not a care in the world, knowing she'd be taken care of. Why hadn't

Anna seen this before? All the time Josephine had appeared to be helping, she had been only doing what didn't seem too difficult. Anna knew it was completely and totally up to her to make things right. And so far, she hadn't been successful.

Anna forced herself to turn down the street where the undertaker's establishment stood. Her hand shook as she turned the doorknob and entered the gloomy parlor. Mr. Fletcher mysteriously appeared from behind a heavy velvet curtain and motioned her to take a seat. Speaking matter-of-factly, as though her father died every day, he launched into a detailed explanation of how he had already laid her father's body in a plain pine coffin.

Another expense we can ill afford, Anna thought as she struggled to stay her tears.

At last the undertaker rose from the seat he had occupied opposite Anna's, signaling an end to his morose speech. Magnanimously, he offered to show Anna her father's body, but she knew that with just one glimpse of her father's lifeless form, she would certainly lose control of her fragile emotions. She could ill afford to break down now. She made a hasty retreat toward the door, announcing that she would send word tomorrow concerning the burial arrangements.

With a heavy heart and a jumbled mind, Anna headed back to the house. The decision she must make concerning her father's final resting place seemed almost insignificant compared to the other crushing crises she faced. She had enough food for the evening meal, but after that, she had no idea what she'd do. The grocer would allow her to return tomorrow for a week's worth of provisions, but how would she pay him at the end of the week? The workers hadn't been paid yet, and the money from the previously harvested fruit still wasn't due for weeks.

When she arrived, Anna was shocked at all the activity around the house and yard. "What is going on?" she demanded when she came upon a woman who was hanging laundry out to dry.

"We're from Good Shepherd Church, and we're here to see to it that you and your mother are well taken care of," the woman said as she continued to hang the freshly washed clothes on the line.

"B–but I never spoke to anyone about this. Who is in charge?" Anna nervously looked around. The only person she knew of who went to that small church was Mr. Hopkins. *Mr. Hopkins! He's the one who organized this.* And, without her permission. *Who does he think he is?*

With her jaw set in determination and her eyes narrowed from anger, Anna set out to find the man who needed to explain what in the world was going on. She wasn't about to continue accepting charity, even when she didn't ask for it. Even though she knew she needed it.

Another group of women stood around the tables on the side lawn. There were deep dishes filled with all sorts of food: meat, vegetables, breads, and desserts. Anna's mouth watered at the aroma that wafted through the cool air. She sure was hungry. Last time she'd eaten was last night, when Mr. Hopkins had come with those men.

After asking someone from every group, Anna learned that Mr. Hopkins had sent these people but hadn't come himself. She also began to suspect that his church wasn't as small as he'd led her to believe. She'd never seen so many do-gooders in her life as were on her property right now.

Josephine came outside and stood on the front porch, watching in fascination as people scurried about. Anna waved, and Josephine lifted her fingers, waving back.

With a heavy sigh, she just shook her head. This was one time she didn't have the energy to stop any-one—not after her unsuccessful day in town. At least, she could save the food she'd bought to cook for to-morrow's dinner.

By the time the workers came in from the groves, they were famished. One look at the spread on the tables, and the prayers started. Anna cringed as she realized she and her mother were the only ones who never said prayers of thanksgiving. But what had God done for them besides take away the head of their household? She wouldn't begrudge the workers their faith, but she wasn't about to give in yet.

The workers had all eaten and taken some food for

their families when Mr. Hopkins finally arrived. He came with a smile on his face and more food in his saddlebags. "Was there enough for everyone?" he asked.

"Yes, thank you," Anna said coolly. "You really didn't have to go to such extremes."

"I know that," he said, without letting her dissuade him from his intentions. "But the Lord is pleased when we take care of others."

"Maybe you can convince me of that someday," Anna said as she looked around at the grapefruit-filled trees lining the lawn. "But at the moment, things look pretty bleak."

"They often do before He shows us where He wants us to go."

Anna snorted as she shook her head. "All I know is that my mother and I lost my father yesterday, and we're about to lose everything else today. What more could He possibly want?"

"Perhaps for you to sit still, pray, and listen to what He has to say?" Mr. Hopkins offered gently and with conviction.

"Ha!" Anna picked up a plate and offered it to him. "Fix yourself something to eat. Have all you want. We're especially generous on this glorious day." The sarcasm dripped from her voice, but she couldn't help it. She was hurting inside.

"Sit down, Anna. I think we need to talk."

She numbly did as she was told.

Daniel Hopkins sat across the table from her and

leaned forward. "Okay, first of all, I want to get a few things straight, Anna. I am not your enemy. I'm here to help you as a friend. And I must insist that you call me Daniel. 'Mr. Hopkins' is getting old."

In spite of the ache deep in her heart, Anna offered him a bitter smile. She had to admit, Daniel sure would be a whole lot easier to say. "Okay, Daniel. What else would you like from me?"

"Nothing."

"Nothing?" she questioned as she stood back up. "Come on, Mr., er. . .Daniel, everyone wants something."

"Like I said, nothing. Everything the good Christian people from my church are doing is because they love Jesus." After a moment's hesitation and a deep breath exhaled, he continued. "All of us have experienced something in our lives, some tragedy that could have turned us away from the Lord."

"H–have you?" Anna stuttered, so stunned by his bluntness, she wasn't quite sure what to do.

Daniel sniffed and nodded his head. "As a matter of fact, yes. I lost my father to a band of thieves when I was merely a boy of thirteen. They left us with nothing, not even the shirts on our backs. After that, it was up to me to take care of my mother and sister."

"I–I'm sorry," Anna apologized, not knowing what else to say after such an open admission. "I had no idea."

"What's more," he added, his voice gruff, "they left us all with ugly scars and more fear than you can ever imagine. If it weren't for the good Lord guiding people from the church to us, we might have been left to starve, not only for food but for His word."

Anna couldn't take her eyes off the man who'd just exposed his soul to her. He'd endured much more than she ever had. "How did you become a successful businessman?"

"With the Lord's blessing, I worked hard; starting with nothing but the willingness to do whatever I had to do. It took years for me to acquire what I have today. It wasn't easy. I understand your pain, Anna, and I can certainly sympathize. In fact, I went through quite a bit of anger myself when I was old enough to realize what had happened to my family. Fortunately, the Christian leaders were patient with me, and their prayers brought me to the Lord. It wasn't easy for any of us. But, today, I know where everything comes from, thanks to that horrifying experience."

Anna swallowed hard. If what he was telling her was true, he did know what her pain felt like. At least, he was consistent. She'd never seen anyone so adamant about anything in her life. Most people would have backed down by now. And, she had to admit, she didn't know anyone else who'd been through anything nearly as dreadful as what Daniel had just told her.

Maybe it *was* time for her to listen. If Daniel Hopkins had something worthwhile to say, perhaps she would be able to do something to save the homestead. He was, after all, a successful businessman and community leader. "Okay, Daniel, what do you suggest I do to keep from having to sell the farm?"

He studied her for a moment, then motioned for her to sit back down. Once she did, he sat down beside her. Placing both of his hands over his heart, he said, "Do you know what I'm feeling right now?"

"Your heart?" she asked. Her own heartbeat raced as the question escaped her lips and a strange emotion swept through her, making her feel weak inside.

"Yes."

Anna nodded. "But, why?"

He balled his hands into a fist and gently pounded his chest. "This is a heart filled with the love of Jesus Christ my Savior. He lived and died for me so that I may experience the salvation that I don't deserve."

"What's the point of all this, Daniel?" Anna asked. She could tell that he was trying to prove something, but she preferred the direct approach.

"The point of all this, Anna, is to show you that you can't do it all alone. The way I see it, your father was a very shrewd businessman who didn't mind taking chances. They were calculated risks, that's for certain, and as long as he lived to see them through to the end, everything was all right. But now, he's gone, and you're stuck with one of his risks—stuck right smack dab in the middle."

"All right," Anna agreed, "I'll grant you that. But what is your point?"

"As a Christian, it's my job to show you the love of Someone who was nailed to the cross for you."

Anna shook her head. "I'm not sure if I believe I'm worthy of something so big as all that."

With a huge smile, Daniel jumped up and shouted, "You're right! You're *not* worthy!"

He must be insane, Anna thought. One minute he was telling her that Jesus had died for her, and the next, he was saying she didn't deserve it. "Are you having trouble making up your mind, Daniel?" she asked with a chuckle. "Or is this some kind of game we're playing?"

"No," he said very solemnly. "This is definitely not a game. This is eternity. This has to do with forever and ever."

"But what about tomorrow?" Anna asked.

Again, he nodded. Anna braced herself for another tirade, but it didn't come. This time, he just said, "We'll take care of today's troubles today and tomorrow's troubles tomorrow, Anna. But we have to trust Jesus for anything beyond that."

"I sure do wish it was that easy," she said with a sigh. "All I want is to keep this farm."

"There are no guarantees in this life, Anna," he stated. "I'll do everything I can to help you. I don't know the first thing about harvesting citrus, but I can try."

"You'd do that for me? You'd actually help me, even after all the things I've said to you?" she asked.

"Yes, I would. In fact, I insist on helping you."

"But I can't promise to have the same love for the Lord that you do." She narrowed her gaze and stared at him, willing him to back down.

"I realize that, but I also know what you're going through right now. You're angry with God for taking away someone you love. I'm surprised you're still fighting so hard and not crying your heart out in a room all by yourself."

"Maybe that'll come later," Anna admitted. She felt like hiding and crying at the moment, yet she knew that would only delay what she had to do. "But first, I have to make sure that everything my father lived for doesn't all get sold to the highest bidder."

Chapter 4

Daniel sucked in a deep breath, wondering how he should proceed. She was still so angry; she was lashing out at whatever was convenient at the moment. Now he had a better understanding of why James had wanted to wait to share with his wife and daughter about his recommitment to Christ. Their anger was deep.

After a few seconds of pondering the right thing to do, Daniel decided it was time to gently back away from the spiritual discussion. No sense in giving her another reason to be angry with God. She'd already justified her feelings in her own mind, and he suspected this would only fuel the fire. He wouldn't let up on witnessing about his faith—but right now he needed to let the Lord do His quiet work in Anna's heart.

"Why don't I stop by the house and take a look at your books, Anna? That way I can get an idea of what we're dealing with from a business perspective." He stopped talking and waited for her to reply.

She hesitated. He knew she didn't completely trust him, but what choice did she have? Even if she was a genius at bookkeeping, none of the businessmen she needed to work with would take her seriously, simply because she was a young woman. They would listen to him.

Slowly, Anna nodded. "I don't suppose there would be anything wrong with that, Daniel."

He gently placed his hand on her shoulder and looked into her eyes. "You can trust me, Anna. I have no intention of ever bringing harm to you or your mother." Her softness and vulnerability made him want to pull her to his side and protect her. But he knew such a gesture was inappropriate now.

She licked her lips and blinked a few times. Daniel knew this was perhaps the most difficult thing she'd ever had to do in her life. He watched as she contemplated the alternatives. It didn't take her long to agree. "I know I can trust you, Daniel," she whispered softly. "I don't know how I know, but I do."

Nothing she could have said would have brought more joy to his heart. All he'd asked of her was for her trust, and now she'd given it. Daniel's heart was melting around this woman. He knew that her worldly vulnerability was only temporary. She was strong. But she also needed to recognize her spiritual weakness, which was the only thing standing in the way of her contentment.

Then, there was the issue of coming to terms with her father's death, which was something she hadn't yet allowed herself to face. The grief she would face, after she got past this hurdle of keeping the grove, would overwhelm her. Then she would need him once again. He was convinced of that. He wouldn't let her down then, either. The Lord had never let him down at times like this, so he knew he was armed with what he needed to help her.

"Would you like for me to go over the books to-night, or should I return tomorrow?" he asked.

Anna smiled, her face still somewhat guarded but not as hard as before. "You don't believe in wasting time, do you?"

"No, not at a time like this," he replied. "We have something else we need to deal with, too, Anna. Your father's burial."

She swallowed hard as the tears sprang to her eyes. "I–I'm not sure what to do about that," Anna said. "My mother and I haven't really discussed it."

"Tell you what, Anna," he said. "Talk with your mother about it this evening. Tell her about the church's offer. This will make everything much simpler all the way around."

"Yes, I can see where it would," she said. "I'll speak to her."

Daniel didn't want to overwhelm her. Besides, she needed some time alone with Josephine. "I must leave now, Anna. I'll be back tomorrow morning after I finish my own business in town."

❧

Why Anna felt that she could trust Daniel now was

something she didn't understand. But she did trust him. So far, he'd been true to his word. She bid him good-bye, then headed upstairs to speak with her mother.

Josephine was in bed when Anna got to the door of her room. "Mama, we need to talk."

"Come on in," Josephine replied weakly. Her face was still pale. She looked so fragile, Anna was afraid she might break, so she walked softly across the room and stood beside her mother's bed. "What did you need to discuss?"

This was difficult for Anna. She didn't want to always have to bring up distasteful conversations, but they did need to decide what to do about her father.

"Where are we going to bury Daddy?" Anna asked.

Josephine's eyes widened with surprise, and then she looked down at the sheets. "I'm not sure. I thought you had already taken care of the matter."

"How could you think that, Mama? I can't make all these decisions on my own!" Before Anna had a chance to catch herself, she'd blurted out what she'd been thinking. She had to take a step back to keep from falling over backwards; she was so weak with the turmoil inside her head and her heart.

Josephine shrugged and looked away. "I just always thought those things kind of took care of themselves."

Anna had always known her mother didn't have a mind for business. She was also rather fragile, which was why Anna was an only child. Now, Anna knew that she was in the position of taking care of her mother. Her own feelings would have to be dealt with later.

"What would you like for me to do, Mama?" Anna asked, knowing it was a moot point.

As her hand brushed the wisps of hair from her face, Josephine replied, "Anna, darling, would you mind taking care of this for me? I have no earthly idea what to do in times like this. I—I've never had to make funeral arrangements before."

"Sure, Mama. I'll take care of everything." Anna backed toward the door before she thought to add, "Mr. Hopkins will be back tomorrow to look over Daddy's books."

Josephine grinned in the beatific way she always had. "He's such a nice boy, Anna. I think he may be sweet on you."

"I don't think so, Mama." Anna stood and looked at her mother for a long second before turning and practically running to her own room. She needed to get away from her mother's watchful eye, for it completely confused her. One minute, Josephine seemed unaware of everything going on around her. The next, she seemed so astute. The very idea of Daniel being sweet on Anna brought a flush to her cheeks.

Anna had to admit, whenever Daniel was in her presence, her heart hammered twice as hard, and she was certain twice as loud. There was a kindness coupled with his masculinity that reached a place inside her—a place she hadn't even known existed before now. She fell asleep wondering what it would feel like to be wrapped in his loving embrace.

The next morning, Anna awoke remembering Daniel's promise to return. She rose, dressed, and rushed around the house to make it presentable. Less than a month ago, her father had dismissed the household servants, saying, "There are only three of us, Anna, so it shouldn't be any problem for you to maintain this place. It's big, but we only live in a few rooms, anyway. You can take care of it, at least until we receive payment for the grapefruit."

Anna had agreed, being the practical sort that she was. And her father was right. It didn't take her long to get the place looking spic-and-span.

Daniel arrived late morning, just like he'd promised he would. She directed him to her father's study, opening his ledger books for him and showing him where everything was. "And he kept all correspondence in this drawer," she added, pointing to the right-hand side of the desk. "The key is in the top drawer."

He smiled up at her. "Why don't you go on about your business, Anna? Unless I have any questions later, I don't think you need to remain in here." His gaze dropped. "Unless, of course, you want to."

Anna did want to, but she knew he'd be able to study the books much more thoroughly without her there. "No, I need to see about the farmhands now. I'll be back this afternoon."

Daniel nodded. Anna looked at him one more time

before turning and leaving him alone in her father's study, gently closing the door behind her. Then, she shut her eyes as her memory of last night's thoughts and feelings toward Daniel returned. Suddenly, a lightning bolt of longing charged through her.

She went out to the edge of the field where the bushel baskets were lined, waiting to be filled with the grapefruit her father had planted several years ago. Fortunately, the oranges were almost all harvested, so they only needed to gather the grapefruit. The process had been a long and arduous one, which was risky at best. But, based on the number of orders they'd already received, it would pay off in large sums—if only the businessmen in town had confidence in her ability to run the farm.

One of the workers had just come in from picking. "Miss Drake," he said in his heavy accent, "some of the workers didn't show up today. They are saying that you cannot pay us our wages."

Anna gulped. She had expected this sooner or later, but she had hoped it would be after Daniel offered her some advice. "Please give me a few days, Miguel," she said in as firm and confident a voice as she could, given the circumstances. "I will have your wages for you then."

He tried to smile. Then he looked down at his shoes, with holes large enough for his toes to poke through. "I have a family, Miss Drake. I cannot afford to go too much longer without my pay."

"I understand, Miguel. Please tell the other workers

who have remained that I will make sure they receive their wages."

"I will tell them," he said as he turned to go back to his work. "It must be soon, or we will have to look for other work."

The second he was out of sight, Anna's legs threatened to give out beneath her, forcing her to sit. She understood their plight, but she had no idea how she'd cover their wages. The only money they had was in her bag, and it wasn't even enough to feed her workers a complete meal. How would she manage to pay them, unless Mr. Blankenship gave her a short-term loan?

She sat there on the ground, looking out over the groves her father had planted, knowing his hopes had been for a large return on his investment. The only hope she now had was in the hands of the man sitting in her father's study right now. Was there anything Daniel could do, short of asking God for a miracle?

When Anna's strength returned, she slowly stood up, being careful not to fall back down. She needed to drink something. Her mouth was parched.

As she headed back toward the house, she thought of Daniel Hopkins and how he'd talked so openly about his faith. He had known her father, but she could not for the life of her figure out how.

Evidently, if Daniel's words were true, he had held more than one discussion with her father about spiritual matters. Moreover, Daniel had spoken of her father's decision to recommit his life to Christ. Yet, as far as

Anna knew, James Drake wasn't a godly man. If her father had gone back to church, it must have been on one of those Sunday mornings when she'd been allowed to sleep late, which had happened a few times since the grapefruit trees had been planted.

When she went inside, Daniel was standing by the window. She could tell he'd been watching her. Had he been there watching her when her legs had nearly buckled?

Chapter 5

Anna knew the answer to her question as soon as she acknowledged him. "Are you feeling ill, Anna?" he asked, a grave expression on his face. She couldn't tell if it was from concern for her or from something he'd found in her father's books.

"I–I'm not now," she replied. "Ever since Daddy died, I sometimes feel weak at the knees."

His face relaxed and he smiled, so she knew that his tense expression was out of concern for her. "I've read some of the correspondence as well as looked at the figures in the ledgers."

"Yes?" she said, anxious to know what he'd come up with.

"Your father was an excellent businessman. He only left one thing up in the air, and that was what would happen to the business if he were incapacitated."

"Or dead," she added, nodding, her heart still aching. She knew that he wanted to soften the reality of the situation, but she needed to hear the truth.

"Yes," he agreed, nodding, "or dead." He began pacing, rubbing his chin as he walked back and forth across the floor between her and the window, stopping every couple of times to look outside.

"Okay, Daniel," she finally said. She couldn't stand not knowing the verdict. "What did you find?"

"I can only see two choices for you and your mother, Anna, and I'm afraid you won't care for either of them." He looked her in the eye, almost as if he needed to evaluate her reaction before telling her what he knew.

"Tell me. Please." Anna sat down in the chair beside the window. She was afraid that once she heard what he had to say, her knees might grow weak again. Daniel had already seen her collapse too many times.

"All right," he finally said, "here it is. Your father purchased the grapefruit trees with money he had stashed away from last year's orange profits. Naturally, I assumed that he bought them on credit, but he didn't. It actually would have been better if he had because that would have freed up some of the available funds for you to pay your workers."

Anna listened attentively. So far, she understood, so she nodded.

"There are two solutions to your problem." He stopped talking and rubbed his chin again. She surmised he was trying to decide where to begin. "The first one sounds like something you're not interested in pursuing, but I feel like I need to state it. You may sell the groves, with or without the property the house sits on. The only problem with that is that you won't have the means to continue living here. So if you choose this option, it would probably be better to sell the house along with the groves."

Anna squeezed her eyes shut and shook her head. That sounded like the kiss of death to her. She'd never known life outside this farm. This was her home. "And what is the other option?" she asked.

Daniel extracted a letter from a file on the desk. "I never would have thought of this if I hadn't read some of the correspondence in the desk, but I feel that it is an excellent solution to your problem. Your father had been working on plans to deed some of the land to his workers in exchange for their labor on the land he continued to personally hold."

"I–I don't understand," Anna stuttered. "He was thinking of giving our land away? That makes no sense. Daddy wouldn't do that."

Daniel held his hands up. "It's actually pretty simple," he said. "Let me explain a little more. You and your mother currently own more than two hundred acres of citrus groves. You may choose to give ten acres to each of the ten workers' families, and you'll still own one hundred acres. If you do that in exchange for the labor, you may not have to come up with the cash to pay them. They will participate in their share of the profits, based on how much their own trees yield."

Anna sucked in a breath and let it out slowly as she thought about this plan. She didn't really like the thought of letting go of so much land, but what choice did she have? "How about living expenses in the meantime?" she asked, wondering what sort of brilliant solution Daniel would have to this problem.

Daniel cleared his throat before he began talking. "I haven't spoken to the congregation at Good Shepherd Church yet, but I was thinking that we might want to help you and your workers out for a while longer, at least until you receive payment on the firstfruits of your labor."

Anna's eyebrows sprang up in surprise. "You think they'd want to do that?"

He smiled. "I'm sure they'd consider it."

As much as Anna hated the idea of accepting charity, the alternative sounded even worse. Then she thought of something that would make it seem less one-sided. "How about if we provide the people of Good Shepherd all the grapefruit and oranges they can eat?"

The corners of Daniel's eyes crinkled as he tilted his head back and belted out a hearty laugh. "I'm sure they'd love that," he replied when he regained his composure. "You sure know how to sweeten the pot, Anna."

If anyone else had laughed at something she'd said, she probably would have gotten angry. But when Daniel laughed, he had a way of making her feel like he was laughing with her rather than at her. His tenderness and sensitive manner gave her a sense of peace. She smiled. "I don't want to owe anyone anything."

That was when his laughter stopped. His expression

became very serious as he said, "We are all debtors, Anna. Christ paid our debt of sin with His sinless life."

Anna gulped. It always came back to this with Daniel, didn't it? It wasn't as if she didn't believe in God. She most definitely did. His presence was obvious as she looked around her. What she had a difficult time understanding was how tragedy could happen to good people and how God could do something like send His only Son to die for her. She was an insignificant creature in the big picture. But Daniel seemed convinced that that wasn't so. So convinced, in fact, that he almost had her believing it, too.

Anna leaned back in her chair and thought for a moment before saying, "I don't want you to think I don't appreciate all you've done for my mother and me, but I do have a question."

"And that is?" he said, tilting his head and giving her his full attention.

"Why are you doing so much?"

"I'm not sure I understand the nature of such a question," he said, appearing to Anna that he was stalling for time.

"I've already told you that I'm angry with God. You're a devoted Christian who goes to church every Sunday. You follow His teachings and seem to desire to hold Him close to your heart. Why would you bother with someone like me?"

He nodded in understanding. "It's very basic, really, Anna. In spite of your anger, you are one of Christ's children. Think of Him as your Father in Heaven. When a man's children disobey, even if it's intentional, does he stop loving them?"

"N—no, I guess not," she replied. Anna remembered all the times she'd disobeyed her father, and although he'd disciplined her, she'd never doubted his love.

"It's essentially the same thing, only more so. Christ loves all people, and He desires our respect and reverence in return. I do it out of love for Him, Anna."

She glanced down at her hands folded in her lap. "I see." It surprised Anna to realize that she'd been hoping for another reason—perhaps that he was interested in pursuing more than a friendship with her. Each time she saw him, her heart skipped a beat.

Daniel paused, then said, "Why don't you come over here and take a look at these books?"

Anna stood up, hesitating for a moment. "I've already looked at them once." Did she dare get close to him?

"Let me show you a few things you may have missed."

She crossed the room and stood beside him, all too aware of his size in contrast to hers. While she stood just a fraction of an inch above five feet tall, he towered over her with at least a six-foot frame. His dark hair also contrasted her honey-blond tresses, which she had twisted into a knot on top of her head. Anna started to reach out to feel his shoulders, but she quickly pulled her hands down to her sides. Now wasn't the time. Maybe later.

Daniel ran his finger along one of the lines in the ledger book. "This is your profit if you keep the entire grove intact." Then, he moved his finger to another line. "And this is your profit if you offer one hundred acres to your workers."

She noticed those two different amounts. "Why isn't that number double this one?" she asked.

"Because we're having to subtract the wages of the workers. Your father apparently intended to pay them partly in land because most of the remainder of this ledger is reflecting the sales from one hundred acres."

Anna sighed. She'd looked at the books, but she hadn't seen what Daniel had seen. Now she felt more inadequate than ever. "I wonder if he spoke to the workers about this," she said.

"You should ask them," he replied. "That is, if you intend to make this offer. Otherwise, you might want to keep it between us."

"I don't know what to do."

"I'm sure there's no hurry," Daniel said as he closed the book. "You might want to sleep on it and ask them tomorrow."

"If I don't do something soon, I'm afraid I may lose more workers. Two families have already left. According to Miguel, the one my father put in charge, they've accepted positions on neighboring farms."

"Would you like for me to talk to them?" Daniel asked.

Anna took a step back and studied his face. His lips

were slightly parted, his hair was tousled from raking his fingers through it, and his sleeves were still rolled to his elbows, making him more attractive than she'd remembered him being. Seeing him concerned about her welfare touched her heart in a way it had never been touched before. She sensed that he really did care about her. *Could the Lord possibly have something to do with these feelings?*

"I think I need to talk to them," she finally replied, "but I would appreciate it if you were nearby for moral support."

He grinned, flashing his crooked smile that made her insides churn. Anna found herself weak at the knees once again.

"I'll be more than happy to be with you, Anna. If you need me to say something, I will. If not, I'll keep my mouth shut."

Anna would have been satisfied with that, so when he cupped his hand around her elbow and led her over to the couch, she looked up at him questioningly. His breath fanned the hair around her face, warming her from the inside out. If he hadn't been supporting her arm, she would have surely fallen to the floor, only this time her weakness resulted from his touch. She wanted to stay close to him, to continue to inhale his masculine scent, to know everything would be fine as she now felt it would be.

"I want you to get some rest. Some members of my church will be by later on with food, so you don't have to worry about that. At least, not now." Daniel leaned down and brushed the stray wisps of hair from her face. His featherlight caress ignited her senses.

Anna nodded and watched him leave; she'd been rendered speechless. Once he was gone, she allowed herself to wonder about her feelings.

What she felt for Daniel still didn't negate the fact that her father had just died. She longed for the man she'd always depended on since birth, but she knew that there wasn't a thing she could do about that longing. She also wondered what her father would have wanted done regarding his burial, but from what she knew, he hadn't made any prior arrangements. Should she take Daniel up on his church's offer of having the funeral at Good Shepherd Church?

When she felt certain that her legs could carry her across the room, she stood up and went over to her father's desk. She opened the drawer that was filled with correspondence. Then, she pulled the letters out, one by one, glancing at the return addresses, wondering what all he had had going on in his life.

She stacked them according to their intended purpose. Each stack seemed to reach into a different part of his life. The largest one was related to business, of course, and she saw how he'd taken one calculated risk after another to achieve a certain level of financial success. It irked her that he was willing to put the house on the line like he had.

The second stack was letters from personal friends.

She didn't care to read much in those because they weren't issues that interested her. She included some of the political letters in that stack because it seemed that her father's interest in government was more of a personal issue than business.

It was the third stack that had her baffled. Most of them were from Good Shepherd Church. Several of the letters were from the old pastor, and a couple were from Daniel, proving that her father had known him before he'd died. Was that why Daniel had been the one to break the sad news? Had Daniel and her father been close friends without her knowledge?

Anna's fingers quivered as she pulled the letter from the envelope. As she read, her heart pounded. It spoke of Daniel's joy over her father's decision to return to church and to bring his wife and daughter so that they, too, might hear the Good News of eternal salvation.

The letter fell from her hands to the desk as she pondered what she'd just read. Perhaps Daniel was right. Her father *had* become a Christian, and he just hadn't yet found the chance to tell her. According to Daniel's letter, her father had intended to go back to the church and eventually include his wife and daughter. The words about concern over Anna and Josephine's lack of faith worried her, too. Was that why her father hadn't shared his newfound belief with his family? *It must be,* she thought. There was no other explanation.

Anna was now more confused than ever about what to do. But one thing was certain: This new knowledge made it much easier to speak to Daniel about the church service and burial for her father. At least she wouldn't feel that she was being a hypocrite. If her father had intended to join the church, then why shouldn't he be buried there?

Suddenly, Anna felt a wave of emotion wash over her as the reality of the whole situation came into full view. Anna and Josephine had been left behind by a shrewd businessman with a slew of unfinished business— unfinished business that included his telling them of his recommitment to the Lord. It was up to her to make things right.

Anna had never stopped acknowledging the Lord's presence, although her faith had grown weak. She'd allowed the pain of losing her father to make her angry at God, and this anger had quickly turned to fear of what He might do next.

Daniel had spoken to her with kindness, making her listen with a firm but loving voice. The Lord spoke to her through Daniel, letting her know that He was in control and He'd never let her down. She could see that now.

Her grief welled up in her throat, forcing the tears to flow from her eyes. Anna cried silently at first, her body shaking as the tears formed fresh streams down her cheeks. Then, as the tracks of tears widened, so did the volume of her sobs. Besides her mother, no one else was in the house, so she didn't care.

"Anna." She quickly glanced up to see her mother

standing in the doorway. "May I come in?"

Anna nodded. "Yes, Mama."

Josephine crossed over to the desk and sat down in the armchair beside it. "I'm so sorry I haven't been available to listen to you. I'm just so grief-stricken myself, I don't know what good I'd be."

"I understand, Mama," Anna said, sniffling.

"Have you figured out all the business yet?" Josephine asked.

"Some of it." Anna braced her hands on the arms of her chair as she sucked in a breath, turning toward her mother. "I've just been thinking about Daddy's funeral."

Josephine wiped her forehead with her embroidered handkerchief. "I'm so glad you're taking care of that, Anna. I wouldn't even know where to start."

"We're burying him at Good Shepherd Church."

"Will they let us do that?" Josephine asked with a shaky laugh. "After all, we haven't set foot inside their church."

Anna licked her lips and sniffled again, finally regaining composure. "Jesus still loves us, Mama." The instant she said those words, she knew they were true. Daniel had said them with conviction, and now she knew she could, too.

"How can you be so sure of that, Anna?"

Daniel's words came to her mind, and the strength of her new conviction washed over her. "Mr. Hopkins said that God loves us like a father loves a child. Even when we disobey, He loves us and wants us to come back."

Anna could hardly believe that these words were coming out of her own mouth. Still, she had meant what she said. A sense of relief flooded her veins, washing away all the anger she'd held inside for way too long.

"Mama, I'm going to find my Bible and start reading a little bit each day. Would you like to join me?"

After several long moments of silence, Anna stood up and left Josephine sitting in the study alone. Apparently, the idea was too much for her mother to consider right now. But Anna felt an overwhelming desire to delve into the Word. She simply couldn't sit back and wait for her mother to join her in this newfound hope.

Chapter 6

*H*ave mercy upon me, O God, according to thy lovingkindness: according unto the multitude of thy tender mercies blot out my transgressions. Wash me thoroughly from mine iniquity, and cleanse me from my sin." Psalm 51:1–2.

Anna must have read the verse at least ten times in so many minutes. And each time she read it, she gained a deeper understanding of God's love. Only a father could love a child this much.

She squeezed her eyes shut, thinking about all the times she had denounced God. She'd shoved Him to the back of her mind, thinking she didn't need Him. But now she knew better. Although she had never quit acknowledging His presence, she'd called on Him only when she wanted something from Him.

And the only way she'd be able to be close to Him now was through His Son, Jesus Christ. All the Scriptures that had been marked in her Bible by the women in her family before her related to Christ's forgiveness.

After reading each verse with a mark beside it, she found more comfort.

"All right, Lord," she said aloud, "I know I have sinned by turning my back on You. Please show me the way back to Your path. Lead me to what's right, Lord." As soon as she said those words, she pressed her face into her pillow and began once more to sob.

The tears fell freely, and for the first time in her adult life, Anna knew what it was like to be forgiven and free from sin. Her father had died only a few days ago, yet he had hope because he'd found the way to everlasting life with Jesus Christ. She and her mother only had each other, which was pitiful, because they weren't able to take on the weight of what lay ahead of them. While she knew it wouldn't be easy to let go of her anger, she now had the Lord to help her through it.

That afternoon, Daniel made good on his offer to stand by her side when she told the workers of what her father had wanted to do. She had no doubt that the Lord had brought Daniel into her life to lead her to Him.

Her fears of the workers turning her down were unfounded. They'd all shouted in excitement that this was what they'd always wanted. Several of them fell to their knees in prayer. Daniel joined them.

Before she realized what was happening, Anna was holding hands, forming a circle with Daniel and all the workers, praying for guidance during this trying time. Daniel closed the prayer, thanking God for His blessings.

When Anna said, "Amen," Daniel squeezed her hand. She felt a rush of energy wash over her.

"Have you decided what to do about your father?" he asked. "He needs to be buried right away. We've waited much too long already."

Anna nodded. "I'd like to lay him to rest in your church cemetery," she said. "That is, if the offer is still open."

"Yes," he said with a sensitive smile, "the offer is still open. I've already spoken with the men of the church about it, and they agree. Your father was in the process of talking to them about joining the flock, so we feel that this is fitting."

"Will there be a good time for me to talk with someone about joining the church myself, Daniel?" she said softly, barely able to hear her own words. "I know I still have quite a bit to learn, but I'm willing."

Daniel turned and looked at Anna with pure, unadulterated joy on his face. "Anytime is good when you make this kind of decision, Anna."

Anna breathed a sigh of relief. Everything was now going quite well. "I don't know how to thank you," Anna said as they strolled back to the house.

"But, Daniel, I have one more problem I need your advice on. . ." She paused as she pondered how to put forth the question. Finally, she let the words tumble freely. "I feel as though I need to tell my mother about Daddy's newfound faith—and mine. However, I'm afraid she'll think I'm preaching at her. Or even worse, judging her. What should I do?"

Anna's mouth suddenly went dry. She licked her lips. "What should I say?"

He shrugged. "Anna, I suggest you share your own personal experience with her to start."

"I don't think she'll understand," Anna said as dread washed over her. "Besides, if I say the wrong thing, I might mess everything up."

"Trust me, Anna. Whenever you speak of the Lord from your heart, He's right there beside you. He makes a promise, I believe it's in 1 Peter, verse fifteen: 'Sanctify the Lord God in your hearts: and be ready always to give an answer to every man that asketh you a reason of the hope that is in you with meekness and fear.'"

Anna slowly nodded. She'd read that verse. In fact, she'd read quite a bit of the New Testament last night. That was why she was so exhausted. She hadn't gotten much sleep.

Later that night, when all was quiet around the house, Anna went to her mother's bedroom door and knocked. "Mama, is it all right if I come in?"

"Of course, Anna," Josephine said softly. "The door isn't locked."

This was perhaps the most difficult thing she'd ever had to do. Witnessing to anyone would be trying, but witnessing to her mother would surely prove the hardest. After all, this was something most parents talked about with their children, rather than the other way around. Josephine was sitting in front of her mirror brushing her hair. She was such a lovely woman, and Anna rarely saw her with her hair down around her shoulders. It made her look years younger.

"Mama, have you considered going back to church?" Anna finally asked, after building up enough nerve.

Josephine held her brush away from her head and turned to face Anna. "Why, no, sweetheart. Your father and I had this very same conversation a few weeks ago. I'll tell you the same thing I told him. I like to sleep in on Sunday mornings. Going to church seems like such a waste of time."

"Daddy wanted you to go to church with him?" Anna asked in disbelief. "Why didn't you tell me?"

Josephine shrugged as she resumed brushing her hair. "I didn't think it all that important. Besides, what good did it do your father? He'd started attending services again, and now he's gone."

"But what if he hadn't renewed his relationship with the Lord?" Anna said, still stunned by this new revelation. "He would have died anyway, and we wouldn't have had a peace about his salvation."

"Is this important to you, Anna?" Josephine asked, still smiling.

"Yes, Mama, it is," Anna replied. "Very important, as a matter of fact."

"Then if you want to attend church services, why don't you go with that nice young man Daniel who keeps coming around the house? I have a feeling he'd like to court you."

"Mama," Anna said as she came closer to her mother. She squatted down beside her and took the brush from her mother's hand. "I really want you to go with me."

"No, Anna," Josephine said, standing up and turning to face her daughter. "I won't go. If you want to, that's fine. But leave me out of it. If God had spared your father, I might have gone with him eventually, but I don't want any part of church if this is the kind of god they worship there."

Anna paused, then stood up, backing toward the door. "Jesus loves you, Mama. He loves you in spite of what you just said. And if it weren't for His love, we might just as well have starved to death." As soon as she'd spoken those words, she turned and fled from her mother's room to her own room at the other end of the hall.

The instant she was inside her bedroom, Anna flung herself across her bed, tears streaming down her face. "Oh, Lord. I don't know how much more I can take."

She fell asleep still dressed. When she awoke, she felt as though she'd been up all night.

Daniel arrived in the early afternoon. "I want to study your father's books a little bit more. Perhaps there's one more thing we can do to bring in some extra cash."

"By all means, please do whatever you can," Anna said in a monotone.

"What's wrong, Anna?" Daniel asked as she turned her back on him. He reached out and turned her back around to face him. His face was so close she could feel his breath. She sucked in some air and held it for what seemed like hours. "Anna?"

Anna wasn't sure if he pulled her to his chest or if she fell against it. All she knew for certain was that she was leaning against his strength, both physically and emotionally, and he didn't back away. He was rock solid, and she was grateful.

"Anna, darling, I'm so sorry."

"What are you sorry about?" she asked. "You did nothing wrong."

"I'm sorry about whatever is troubling you. Would you like to tell me about it?"

He kept his arm around her, most of her weight supported by him, as they made their way over to the couch, where he slowly lowered both of them to a sitting position. Brushing her hair from her face, he cupped her face in his hands. "Please tell me."

Anna began telling him about how, long ago, her father had decided that attending church was a waste of time and that he didn't need God in his life. As she explained how she, her mother, and her father would all be in the same house, yet never even acknowledge the others' presence, she realized, for the first time, how odd this must seem. She finished by telling him what had happened last night.

"The whole encounter was awful, Daniel," Anna said as she lowered her face to his shoulder. "My mother all but denied the deity of the Lord."

"Anna, we can't force your mother to believe. At this point, all we can do is pray."

He gently stroked her head. She pulled away slightly and looked deeply into his eyes. "Anna," he whispered before lowering his face to hers and claiming her lips with his own.

The kiss was sweet and tender, yet it reached all the way to her core. "Oh, Daniel," she muttered, her mind still swirling with the impact of her first kiss.

When they finally broke away from each other's embrace, Daniel rose to leave. His parting words were barely audible as he hurried out the door.

"I'd best be going. We both have work to do."

It wasn't long before the people from the church showed up with food. They had provided meals for Anna, Josephine, and the workers every single day since her father's death. This was a testament of their faith, Anna now realized. She was truly grateful for Daniel, the people of his church, and, most of all, for Christ's love and His never-ending mercy.

The next morning, they buried James Drake in the church cemetery after a simple Christian service. Anna wept, while Josephine allowed only a few tears to trickle down her cheeks. Her chin quivered, but she said nothing. Once the services were over, Josephine asked to be returned home.

Daniel spent the next several weeks between his own business in Orlando and helping Anna run the groves her father had planted. They both learned what they needed to know to keep up with the harvest and shipping, but Anna now realized how much was involved in the business side of the groves.

"I never knew he did all this," Anna exclaimed one day after finishing the last of the invoices to several dozen of their commercial customers.

"I'm sure there were a lot of things you never knew about your father," Daniel said as he kissed her on the forehead. His kisses were coming with regularity now, and each one warmed Anna's heart. She'd never imagined herself feeling this close to any man. Yet in the back of her mind were the nagging thoughts: *There is no future for our relationship. I could never live up to Daniel's expectations for a wife.*

❧

Josephine spent most of her time up in her room, doing little things, like sewing and darning. She rarely offered to help out around the house or with the business, but Anna didn't mind.

"I think it is time for us to speak to your mother again about attending church," Daniel said one day.

"I've tried," Anna replied as she snapped the ledger book shut, "but she's so stubborn."

"So I'm stubborn, now, am I?" The voice came from the other side of the room.

Anna and Daniel both jerked their heads around to see Josephine standing in the doorway to the study. Her expression was cool and stern, leaving no doubt in their minds how she felt about their discussion of her.

Chapter 7

O h, Mama," Anna said, wishing she'd been more careful with what she said, "that's not what I meant."

"You wouldn't have said it unless you meant it, Anna," Josephine said, her voice as cold as dripping icicles.

Daniel had been glancing back and forth between Anna and Josephine. He finally walked over to where Josephine still stood. "I'm sure our words sounded much worse than we meant them, Mrs. Drake."

"No," Josephine said, slowly shaking her head. "I do have a stubborn streak sometimes, but that's not always bad, is it?"

Anna had no idea how to answer that. If she agreed with her mother, she'd be admitting guilt, but if she didn't, she'd be lying. Fortunately, Daniel spoke up, saving her from having to respond.

"It all depends on what we're being stubborn about," he replied with a chuckle. "But I do know one thing: Your daughter loves you very much, and she is doing everything in her power to make certain this farm stays in the hands of this family."

Josephine's expression instantly turned from aloofness to shock. "Is there any danger of losing the farm?"

"Well, that's always a possibility," Daniel said, in spite of the daggers Anna shot him with her looks. But he went on. "We're having to shuffle things around here quite a bit to get the crop harvested in time to be shipped. There are several hindrances, like spoilage, train and ship schedules, and the fact that we are operating with less hands than we actually need."

"James always said that he used as few workers as he could get away with to keep cost down. Is this a problem now?" Josephine asked, showing an interest in the family business for the first time since her husband's death.

"Yes, Mrs. Drake," Daniel answered, "it is. It wouldn't be if some of the workers hadn't left when we couldn't pay them their wages."

"What about all the money we made on the oranges last year?" Josephine said. "James told me that we did quite well on that crop."

Nodding, Daniel said, "You did, but he spent all the profit on adding more grapefruit trees—and they won't mature for a few years. He was in town working on raising operating capital when he collapsed and died."

Josephine fell back into a chair, letting out a loud sigh. "What will we do?" She sniffled, then said, "I s'pose we could sell this place and buy a house in town."

Daniel glanced over at Anna, who'd just been standing there, taking it all in. She was shocked at how many questions her mother had, as well as how long she'd stuck around after hearing the answers.

Anna finally felt the urge to speak up. "I don't want to do that."

"What will we do then?" Josephine asked weakly.

"Miguel has told me that he will see to it that all the grapefruit gets harvested, even if it means putting all his children out there working from sunup to sundown. Some of the other workers already have their children working alongside them. Miguel loves this farm."

Josephine nodded. Years ago, Miguel had come to this country from Cuba with his new bride. He'd worked for her husband ever since and was devoted to the Drake family.

"People from the church are willing to help, if needed," Anna added.

With a snicker, Josephine stood and headed toward the door. "Well, I'm certain that you'll figure something out. I'm not the only one in this family known to be stubborn!" She shot a quick glance at Anna then turned abruptly, and left the room.

"We need to pray for my mother, don't we?" Anna stared at the empty doorway where, moments before, her mother had stood.

"That is all we can do."

Together they prayed a prayer for mercy and loving care for Josephine. Then, they asked the Lord to watch over the workers as they harvested the last crop of grapefruit that had to be shipped before they could start receiving payment. Finally, they praised the Lord for all the blessings that continued to flow every day. Anna's own faith was strengthened by prayer. While she still felt as though she had a long way to go, she knew she'd come far already.

"Amen," Daniel said.

He opened his eyes and caught her staring at him, something she'd been doing quite a bit lately. He grinned, leaned over, and kissed her squarely on the lips. Anna grinned back and followed with her own "Amen" before they let go of each other's hands. Her heart was filled with a love for Daniel that was growing every day. In her mind, it was a romantic, Christ-induced sort of love that she had no doubt was right for her. But with all the things she had to take care of and all the worries over the farm, she wasn't at liberty to enjoy the feeling. Besides, she continued to wrestle with the lingering doubt that she could live up to Daniel's expectations. She knew she needed to continue to pray about it, but she couldn't help but worry about their vast differences in spiritual depth and maturity.

Daniel had to go back into town to take care of his own business, which had been practically running itself since he'd been helping her. After he left, Anna went to work on more correspondence that seemed to grow by the day. She'd be glad when this last crop was shipped so she could stop and rest.

Small sums of money had trickled in from the retail customers, but only enough to purchase needed supplies and dole out a paltry sum to the workers. There was barely enough money left over for food, so the members of Good Shepherd Church continued to bring food for the workers. Anna no longer felt that she was imposing since she understood their motives. Besides, she always sent them home with bushels of the fruit that had been harvested that day.

Josephine asked questions on a daily basis now, leading Anna to believe that she might actually have an interest in the business. Anna decided not to press, but she always welcomed any help her mother wanted to give.

One afternoon, right after Daniel had left for Orlando, Miguel rushed into the house without knocking, something he'd never done before. "Miss Drake, come quick! There's been an accident!"

Anna dropped the ledger books she was holding, ran out the door following Miguel, and didn't stop until she reached the edge of the groves, where a small group was standing around an older child of one of the other workers. "What happened?" Anna asked, squatting by the child's side to see a pale face and contorted small frame.

"He fell from one of the trees, Miss Drake," Miguel said, his voice filled with anguish. "It's Maria's son, Pedro."

Maria was Miguel's sister who had come to live

with him and his wife after she became pregnant out of wedlock. Back in Cuba, she'd been turned away from their parents, and she had no place else to go.

Anna glanced over her shoulder and motioned for her mother who had followed Anna from the house, to join her. Josephine hesitated for a moment, then began walking slowly toward the small group.

"Mama, I need your help! I have to ride to town to get a doctor, but I don't want to leave Pedro here without someone who can help him. He needs a blanket."

Josephine's face turned a ghastly shade of white, but she nodded and abruptly turned back to do what she could. Anna instructed the others to let her mother take care of the boy once she returned.

Josephine rushed out with a big blanket and gently placed it over Pedro. She turned to look at her daughter and said, "I'll be surprised if the doctor comes. I doubt if the people of Orlando think any more highly of farmworkers than they did in our last town."

"Dr. Murphy is a Christian, Mama. He won't neglect this child."

"We'll see," Josephine said. "From my experience, people call themselves Christians if they think they'll get something in return."

There was nothing Anna could say in response to that bitter statement. She also knew her mother was remembering the doctor from before—the one who'd allowed the migrant worker to die, just because he wasn't in the same social class. So she moved as fast as she could to get help. She sure did hope her mother was mistaken about the doctor, or Anna would never be able to break through her bitterness.

The trip to town was the longest ride she could remember. It seemed to take forever to reach the house where Dr. Murphy lived and practiced medicine. He was sitting in the front office chatting with the mayor.

"A child of one of our workers has just fallen from a tree, and he's in desperate need of medical care," Anna said, not caring that she interrupted their discussion of town politics. "It looks to me like he may have broken some bones."

Dr. Murphy grabbed his bag, nodded toward the mayor, and said, "I'll be back this afternoon, and we can pick up where we left off."

"For heaven's sake, Edward, it's just a farmworker," the mayor said. "We have more important business to discuss."

Dr. Murphy stopped in his tracks, glared at the mayor, and said, "If you want to count on my support in the next election, I suggest you change your uppity attitude. These workers are the backbone of our city, Mayor." Without waiting for a response, he turned and followed Anna.

They rode back to the farm as fast as they could, never once stopping to talk. It was imperative that they hurry as fast as they could.

By the time they arrived at the farm, Pedro had regained consciousness and was moaning. People were still standing around, not having any idea what to do. "Please stand aside," Dr. Murphy said as he made his way through the crowd to get close to the boy. "I need all the room you can give me."

Everyone, including Anna and Josephine, stood and watched as Dr. Murphy knelt on the ground and examined the child. Finally, he stood up and rubbed his whiskers. "We need to get him to town immediately. He's not in good condition. Is your carriage ready to go, Anna?"

She shook her head. "It will take some time to get it ready, Dr. Murphy," she said.

"He's in no shape to put on a horse," he replied. "Go ahead and get the carriage ready. I'll do what I can here."

Suddenly, the sound of horses' hooves could be heard from the distance. They were heading toward the edge of the grove where everyone was still standing. As they drew near, Anna saw that it was Daniel.

He quickly hopped to the ground and offered his help. "The mayor said there had been an accident here, so I thought I might be of service," he said.

The doctor shook his head. "I guess he wants my vote, after all. Well, after this, I s'pose he's got it."

Dr. Murphy and Daniel carefully lifted Pedro to the back of the carriage, and Josephine offered to ride with them, in case she was needed. Anna got her horse and rode beside Miguel to town, following the carriage.

No one had said much yet because they had no idea

what they were facing. Pedro had just reached his teen-age years, and he was still growing. All the way to town, Anna heard Miguel offering prayers to the Lord for His mercy on the child. She prayed a little bit, too, but she was amazed at how powerful Miguel's faith still was, even after the accident.

They arrived at the small hospital, and the men carried Pedro to the examining room. Josephine remained in the front room with Anna, her face still registering the shock from earlier.

"Mama, he's in good hands now. Dr. Murphy is very good."

"Yes, I know," Josephine replied. "I'm surprised he was willing to come all the way out there, just for a worker."

"He's not just a worker. He's a person. And every person is of value—a child of God." Anna couldn't hold back the tears, now that she had done all she could to help Pedro. "Dr. Murphy understands that, and he's going to use his God-given skills to help Pedro."

"We'll see," Josephine said, this time not quite so sure of her own words.

Dr. Murphy had taken Daniel and Miguel into the examining room with him. Someone had fetched Maria, and she arrived right when the men emerged from the examining room.

"My Pedro," she cried. "Where is he? Is he going to be all right?"

Dr. Murphy swallowed and touched her shoulder. "I'm not sure yet, Maria. He has broken his back, and we won't know the extent of the injuries for a few days."

"Oh, dear God," she cried as her eyes squeezed shut, tears hanging from her eyelashes before they began to form a stream down her cheeks.

Josephine crossed the room and put her arms around Maria's shoulders, steadying the woman so she wouldn't topple over. Maria allowed herself to be guided to a chair, and she sat down.

"Lord, please have mercy on my son," Maria began to pray. She praised God through the entire prayer. Josephine stared at Maria in disbelief. When Maria opened her eyes, she looked at Josephine. "The Lord will look after us."

Josephine narrowed her eyes and said, "Just like that, you think your son will be healed?"

"I'm not sure my son will be healed in his bones," Maria said. "If I have to choose between his faith and his body, I want him to be right with the Lord."

Anna sat there stunned herself, amazed at the quiet strength of this Christ-loving woman. Daniel smiled at Maria and nodded. "You're a good mother, Maria. We'll all pray for Pedro."

Josephine took a few steps back as everyone else began to pray for Pedro. When they were finished, she asked if Anna could take her home now.

Both women were silent all the way to the farm. Anna let Josephine dismount before she took the horse to the barn then returned to the house alone.

When she got inside, her mother had already gone upstairs. Anna felt compelled to speak to her, to find out what was on her mind.

"Mama," Anna said as she knocked on her mother's door.

"What do you want, Anna?"

"I'd like to talk to you."

"There's nothing to talk about." Anna could tell her mother had been crying, so she backed away. They could talk tomorrow.

That evening, some people from the church arrived with food. They had sent someone every day since her father's death, regardless of the weather, to make sure the Drake family and farmworkers ate. This was such an amazing act of human kindness, Anna often found herself without enough words of thanks.

Josephine came down to talk with the men who'd brought the food their wives had cooked. "We may not be needing this food much longer, since it appears we'll be forced to sell our farm."

"What?" Anna said, spinning around in disbelief at what her mother had just said.

"Now that it is becoming apparent that our workers can't possibly bring in all the harvest, I must make a decision soon." Josephine lowered her head and then raised it again with pride. "I will let you know as soon as I've thought things through. Thank you for all you've done." Then, she went back to the house and left Anna standing there with the men, all of them temporarily dumbfounded.

"I–I'm sorry," Anna said when she found her voice again, "but this was the first I heard of this, too. I'm not sure what we'll do, but I have no intention of selling the farm."

The men exchanged glances, then nodded to each other. One of them stepped forward and said, "If it would help, perhaps we can get a group together to help harvest the last of the grapefruit."

Chapter 8

O h, I couldn't ask you to do such a thing," Anna said. "You've done so much to help us already."

"If we gathered a dozen men, we could help the workers who remain. I suppose we could finish it in half the time that the job would take if we didn't help," one of the men said.

Anna shook her head. "I can't allow you to spend that much time away from your own families and businesses."

Another man stepped forward and looked her in the eye. "If this had happened to any one of us, we'd hope that you'd do the same. We're all followers of Christ, and we feel strongly that He'd want us to take care of you and your family."

Tears instantly sprang to Anna's eyes. She gulped as they headed back toward their horses. They'd told her that they were going to help, and she knew they'd be true to their word. The people from Daniel's church were standing behind their proclamation of faith. This was what Josephine needed to see.

"Anna, I don't understand why you're being so stubborn about this place. It's just a house and a bunch of trees. We can sell to someone who knows what they're doing and buy ourselves a cute little place in the city."

"I don't want a place in the city, Mama," Anna replied. "I want to stay here."

Josephine put down the plate she was holding and stared at her daughter. "You and I both know we're living here on borrowed time. It won't be long before we're forced to give it all up. Why not go ahead and do it now?"

"Yes, Mama, you got one thing right. We are living on borrowed time. But not because of this house and the groves. We're living on the time that the Lord has loaned us. I think we'll do just fine once we get through this year. The men from the church have offered to help, and Miguel said he'd find some more workers before next year."

With a look of resignation, Josephine shook her head. "Anna, dear, those men from the church were just talking. They have no intention of actually coming here and doing all that labor. It was an offer they were certain you'd refuse."

"You'll see, Mama," Anna said softly. How could her mother be such a naysayer after all the kind people from the church had done?

Josephine smiled back at her. Anna felt as though she had to hold onto the farm with one hand and conduct an orchestra with the other; her mother was being so difficult. Maybe, once they had the harvest behind them, she and Daniel could convince her to at least try going to church again.

The very idea of going to church with Daniel sent a rush of excitement through Anna. She knew she was in love with him, even if she could never make him a good wife. He exuded a strength of faith through his actions and words unlike anyone she'd ever seen. He never seemed to tire of carrying out God's Word. With a sigh, she imagined herself being with Daniel for the rest of her life.

There was only a week left before the harvest had to be completed. What had been dubbed the "Sunshine Harvest" by her father now seemed like the "Harvest in Darkness" because there was so much uncertainty. Anna knew that the only hope she had of holding onto the farm was to accept the offer made by the men from the church.

With a sigh, she told Daniel, "I feel as though I've depended on others far too much since Daddy died."

"Nonsense," he said as he tenderly touched her face, giving her that warm glow of relief that came from his caresses. "You have done more than any other woman I know. This farm has been placed in your care by the Lord, and I think you're doing a marvelous job."

His confidence in her brought a new sense of joy to Anna. She nodded and smiled. "Without His help, all hope would be lost."

They gazed longingly at each other for a few seconds.

But the spell was broken by Miguel, who began knocking loudly at the front door. "Miss Drake," he hollered, "you need to see this!" It was an unseasonably warm day, and the windows were open, allowing his voice to drift through the house.

Anna's heart almost stopped as she broke away from the man she loved. "What is it, Miguel?" She pulled open the front door to find Pedro sitting at Miguel's feet. Kneeling down, she took the boy's hand in her own. "Pedro," she said softly, "how are you feeling?"

He beamed back at her. "I can walk again, Miss Drake."

Miguel took over for Pedro, explaining, "The doctor said that we can let him take a few steps at a time. We need to be very careful, but the Lord has been very good to us. I wanted you to see this."

"This is wonderful news, Pedro," Anna said to the boy. Then, she looked at Miguel. "Has Mama seen him?"

"No," Miguel said, the smile fading from his face.

"Let me get her." Anna turned to Daniel. "Stay right here, all three of you. I need to get Mama from her room."

"I'll do whatever you need, Anna," Daniel said. Then he bent down and gently laid a hand on Pedro's shoulder.

She ran all the way upstairs to her mother's room and knocked. "Mama, come quick. There's someone downstairs to see you."

"Who is it, Anna?" her mother said as she opened

the door. At least she was dressed.

"You'll see." Anna turned and ran back downstairs, hoping her mother would follow. She did.

"Oh, my!" Josephine exclaimed when they reached the porch. "What in the world are you doing out of bed, Pedro?" she asked the boy, who was beginning to show signs of exhaustion.

"I can walk, Señora," he replied.

Josephine turned to Anna, then Daniel, and said, "Is this all right with the doctor?"

Daniel shrugged. "The doctor told him to try taking a few steps at a time, so I suppose so."

With a sincere smile, Josephine leaned over and hugged Pedro. "I'm so happy for you, Pedro. Just make sure you do what the doctor tells you."

"I will," he said, his eyes huge and round. "We have been praying every day."

Anna watched her mother's lips quiver. This child was a walking, talking testimony, and Anna hoped her mother saw that. But even if the Lord had not chosen to let Pedro walk, Anna knew that He knew what He was doing in a way she might not understand. However, she doubted her mother would see things that way.

Daniel pulled out his pocket watch. "I need to run into town and let the men know their hands will be needed to complete the harvest. They will start first thing in the morning."

"Thank you, Daniel," Anna said, touching his arm tenderly.

Anna knew that her mother saw this exchange, but Anna didn't care. In fact, the whole world could find out how she felt about Daniel, and that would be fine.

Once Daniel, Miguel, and Pedro were gone, Josephine turned to Anna and said, "You must be very careful, dear, to guard your heart. I wouldn't want you to get hurt."

"Mama, I've given my heart to the Lord," Anna said with conviction. "If He chooses to let me fall in love with Daniel, then I'm helpless to stop it."

"How can you forget what happened before?" Josephine asked. "Last time we got involved with Christians, we found out just how unchristian people can be."

"That was a different situation, Mama," Anna said softly. "We can't judge all Christians by the actions of a misguided few."

Josephine issued a cynical cackle. "They certainly did talk about it a lot."

Shaking her head, Anna replied, "Maybe so, but I see a big difference here with Daniel and the others from the church. Yes, he is a part-time preacher, but he doesn't just preach. He lives his faith by doing what Jesus would want him to do."

Josephine clamped her mouth shut. She didn't say a word as she walked away from Anna, leaving many words unsaid between them. *Maybe later*, Anna thought. There was plenty of time for discussion. At least the door had been opened.

True to his word, Daniel arrived before sunrise the

next morning with a dozen men, all of them ready to work the land. They deferred to Miguel, who was still in charge of the harvest. He gave them each instructions before they set about plucking the ripe fruit from the trees and filling the crates. Anna had no doubt that the Lord was in control.

Josephine awoke several hours later to the sound of Anna's humming. "What makes you so chipper at such an early hour?" she asked groggily.

Anna smiled, took her mother's hand, and led her to the window that overlooked the groves. "Look, Mama. The men came today to finish the harvest."

"Well, I'll be," Josephine said in amazement. "I never thought this would happen."

Anna turned her mother to face her. "Mama, you need to learn to trust the Lord."

Josephine turned away from her daughter, but not before Anna saw the tears that sprang to her eyes. She'd had so much to deal with; she wasn't able to fully understand what was happening. But there would be time for that.

At the end of a long, grueling day, the men came to the house lawn where Anna had set out the food they'd brought that morning. After a blessing given by Daniel, they ate heartily, sitting at the tables with the workers who'd been in the Drakes' employ for years. It didn't matter that some of the men were businessmen from town and others were common laborers. They were all children of Christ, worshipping the same Lord, feasting on the same food. This brought joy to Anna's heart.

"Anna," Daniel whispered as he pulled her over to the oak tree that stood majestically in the center of the back lawn, the only tree that didn't bear citrus on the whole property, "we need to talk."

"Yes, Daniel?" she said, her heart pounding at his touch.

He pulled her toward him with one hand and stroked the hair from her face with the other. "I know this isn't the most romantic place to do this, but I'd like to ask you something."

Anna tilted her head to one side and said, "What is it?"

"Will you marry me?" He asked his question with a bluntness that startled Anna, causing her to temporarily lose her speech. "You don't have to answer now," he added. "If you need time to think about it, I understand."

She cleared her throat as her senses began to return. "I could never marry you, Daniel." Anna surprised herself at her response. Yes, she loved him with all her heart, but she simply wasn't good enough to marry someone as great as Daniel.

"Why not, Anna? I love you." The tenderness in his eyes forced her to look away. She couldn't say what she needed to say as long as he was looking at her like that.

"I could never measure up to being your wife, Daniel. You're the first true and perfect Christian I've ever met. I'm not sure I could live with all heads turned my way, everyone expecting me to be as good as you."

"Oh, Anna, my love, I'm far from perfect."

"I haven't seen that, Daniel," she said, daring to glance at him once again.

He sucked in a breath and let it out slowly. "I have my flaws and weaknesses. I've had more than my share of frustrations and anguish over the murder of my own father. It took years of thought and prayers for me to lose the bitterness I once harbored in my heart. It wasn't until I allowed Christ to work His way into my heart that I was able to forgive and get on with my life. Everything I do is to the glory of God."

Anna listened with rapt attention. She never saw the angry side of Daniel, but as he spoke, she knew he was telling her the truth. "Please allow me to think about your proposal, Daniel."

He smiled and took her hands in his. "Let's pray about it right now."

Together they bowed their heads and prayed. Daniel asked the Lord to show Anna direction and assurance as she considered his proposal, that she would know her true worth and value, and that she would sense his sincere love. He prayed that she'd be filled with the peace that passes all understanding. Just then, Anna shuddered as an overwhelming sense of peace flowed through her soul.

When they were finished with their prayer, Daniel squeezed her hand. "I'll continue to pray for you, Anna." Then he added, "And us. Let's join the others."

She smiled at him, knowing that she still needed to work through some things, but now with the help of the Lord. Daniel was truly a remarkable man.

"Mrs. Drake," Daniel said as they started dessert, "I'd like for you and Anna to be my guests in church on Sunday."

Anna turned and looked at her mother for a reaction. After all the help they'd received from these generous people, there was no way Josephine could turn him down gracefully.

Slowly, Josephine nodded. "Why, yes, that would be nice, Daniel. What time should we be there?"

Stifling a smile, Daniel replied, "Arrive at nine. Services begin around ten o'clock, but I'd like for you to meet some of the ladies who have been cooking for your workers over the past few months."

Anna respected Daniel for being so gentle with her mother. She appreciated the fact that he held back the smile, which she could tell was threatening to break through his solemn expression upon Josephine's positive response. He showed himself as a true gentleman by allowing Josephine her dignity.

The guests left immediately after they cleaned up. Anna followed Josephine to the house, where they both dropped onto the couch.

"This has been one very trying day," Josephine said with a sigh.

"Yes, it has," Anna replied. Her mother hadn't done half the work she had, but Anna knew that Josephine's tolerance for work was much lower than her own. "I'm looking forward to church on Sunday."

Josephine flinched. She sat there in silence for a few moments, almost as if she didn't know what to say.

"Mama?" Anna finally said. "Are you afraid?"

With a slight nod, Josephine broke into tears, at first with a silent trickle, then with racking sobs. Between sniffles, she said, "I miss James. Why did he have to die?"

"Oh, Mama," Anna said as she hugged her mother, "I'm sad, too, but the Lord will take care of us."

"Yes, I know," Josephine said, still sniffling. "He already has."

Chapter 9

The sanctuary was filling quickly with people from all walks of life. Daniel sat beside Anna with his hands folded in his lap. He'd asked another of the lay leaders to preach this morning so he could sit with the Drake women.

Anna studied the faces of the people who entered the room, wondering where they would sit for the services. Many of them weren't able to find seats at all, due to the crowd. However, they found places to stand in the back. And others sat in windowsills that were barely big enough for small children.

As the preacher spoke of God's grace and mercy, Anna stole quick glances at her mother. Josephine seemed to hang on every word he said.

Anna's heart quickened as they closed in prayer and Daniel gently placed his hand in the small of her back. "Are you ready to join the others for a picnic, or do you need to get back to the farm?" He was touching her but directing the question to her mother. His proposal of marriage seemed to have been forgotten. Anna sighed. She knew it was too good to be true.

Josephine thought for a moment and smiled. "I think I'd like to join the others for a picnic." Then she shyly glanced down at the ground before looking back at Daniel. "B—but I didn't bring anything. Do you think they'd mind, if I promised to bring two dishes next week?"

This time, Daniel didn't hold back his laughter, which rang right along with the church bells, the sound more like music than laughter to Anna's ears. "You are never required to bring anything, Mrs. Drake. No one is keeping score."

This was like a dream come true for Anna. She sat between Daniel and her mother, enjoying a wonderful meal with fellow Christians. Anna watched as her mother laughed aloud for the first time in a long time. She knew that her heart was finally softening toward spiritual things, and she fully expected her to accept Christ as Savior very soon.

When the festivities began to break up, Daniel escorted Anna and Josephine to their carriage. As Anna climbed into her seat, he leaned toward her, winked, and said, "I love you."

Suddenly speechless, Anna opened her mouth but quickly closed it when words wouldn't come. Daniel kissed her, this time not letting her pull away to keep her mother from seeing their affection for each other. Was it possible that he hadn't changed his mind about wanting to marry her?

Anna giggled when she heard her mother say, "Oh, my!"

"I'd like to accompany you back to the farm," Daniel announced with a grin.

"Oh, really, Daniel," Anna said, "you don't have to do that."

"No," he agreed, "but I'd like to. Besides, I have something I'd like to discuss with you."

Josephine smiled as if she knew some deep dark secret. "Tell him to come along, Anna," she said. "It would be nice to have a man escort us home. You never know about the dangers on the roads these days."

Daniel rode his horse alongside Anna's and Josephine's carriage. He glanced over at Anna and winked, bringing a deep heat to her cheeks. Over the past few months, she'd grown more fond of him than she'd ever imagined possible. Ideas of a future with Daniel had invaded her mind, even when she slept.

Once they arrived at the house, Josephine excused herself and went upstairs. Anna was alone with Daniel.

"You said you wanted to talk to me about something?" she asked, turning toward the window with her back to Daniel.

He nodded. "Yes, Anna, I did say that, didn't I?"

She felt his hands reach out and grasp her shoulders, gently turning her to face him. They were standing only a few inches apart, their faces directly in front of each other. She saw something in his eyes she'd never seen before, something that melted her insides, forcing her to look down at the floor.

"Anna, please look at me." She did. "I have a very important question for you, and I want your undivided attention."

"Yes, Daniel?" she said, allowing her gaze to meet his once again. "What would you like to ask?"

"I'd like to ask for your hand in marriage," he whispered. "You've had more time to think about it, and I'm not so sure I can wait much longer to have you as my wife."

Anna felt her eyes widen in wonder. So, he hadn't changed his mind, after all.

Slowly a smile took over her face, and she found herself pulling him toward her.

He chuckled as he leaned over and brushed a feather-soft kiss across her lips. "I want an answer, Anna."

She shuddered. "Yes, Daniel, I would like to marry you."

Their arms went around each other for a longer, more lasting kiss. Anna knew this would be the first of many. The Sunshine Harvest couldn't compare to the brightness now in Anna's heart.

"Daniel?" Anna asked when they at last pulled away from their embrace.

He gazed at her, love written all over his face. "Yes, sweetheart?"

"What should I do with this farm?"

"What would you like to do with the farm?"

She gulped. "Would it be all right with you if we kept it?"

"Absolutely," he replied. "Do you think your mother would like to take my place in town?"

"Oh, Daniel," Anna said as she hugged him again, "you're so good to me."

"I want you to be happy, Anna."

"We'll have to tell our children about the first Sunshine Harvest of grapefruit," Anna said.

"Yes," Daniel agreed, "we'll tell all eight of them the whole story."

Anna gulped. "Eight?"

He chuckled. "That is, unless you want to try for a dozen."

Anna laughed with giddiness. "No, eight will be just fine."

Every pew in the small church was filled with church members and field workers' families as Anna and Daniel said their vows before God. While Daniel promised to love and cherish her for the rest of his life, Anna felt a sense of peace she'd never known until now. This was definitely the right thing to do; there was no doubt in her mind.

After the wedding, there was a reception feast on the church lawn. Josephine had help from the other ladies of the church in preparing an overabundance of food and desserts. People laughed, ate, and sang as Anna and Daniel lovingly gazed into each other's eyes.

Epilogue

The Sunshine Harvest yielded the first shipment of grapefruit and a larger crop of oranges than James Drake had ever recorded in his ledgers. Anna felt confident that her father would have been proud of her. Daniel did a wonderful job of running the business, but she insisted on knowing what was going on at all times. She knew he understood her need, and he shared every bit of news, both good and bad, which suited her just fine.

The church had grown to a size sufficient for the membership to call a full-time pastor. Daniel was more than happy to hand over the leadership to someone else, but he promised to do whatever was needed to help. Anna and Josephine offered their assistance as well. Daniel and Anna had already begun a Bible study with the migrant workers and that was going remarkably well.

Josephine welcomed Daniel's offer of his house in town. She'd always wanted to be in the middle of the action, and her home was now the frequent meeting place of her many good friends from church.

Shortly after the second crop of trees were planted, Anna waited for all the workers to go back to their houses. When Daniel came inside, she said, "I have some good news, Daniel."

He grinned and kissed her on the lips, something she never grew tired of. "What's that, sweetheart?"

"We're going to have a child sometime during the next harvest."

Daniel pulled Anna into his arms and kissed her tenderly. When he pulled away, he looked into her eyes and said, "I knew the Lord was good. But I never realized how good until you came into my life."

Anna felt the same way. Yes, God had been good to her; there was no doubt in her mind.

DEBBY MAYNE

Debby has been a freelance writer for as long as she can remember, starting with short slice-of-life stories in small newspapers, then moving on to parenting articles for regional publications and fiction stories for women and girls. She has been involved in all aspects of publishing, from the creative side, to editing a national health publication, to freelance proofreading for several book publishers. Her belief that all blessings come from the Lord has given her great comfort during trying times and gratitude for when she is rewarded for her efforts. She lives on the west coast of Florida with her husband and two daughters.

Only Believe

by Janet Spaeth

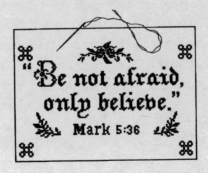

"Be not afraid,
only believe."
Mark 5:36

Chapter 1

"Be not afraid,
only believe."
Mark 5:36

Dakota Territory, 1879

Catherine stared at the heap of metal and leather. This was probably the equipment she needed to harvest Andrew's fields. Then again, it might just be what he used to plant. Or maybe it was all the same gear.

She sighed. She had no idea.

From the nearby stall, a horse whinnied a greeting, and Catherine turned to see the huge animal's velvety gray nose nudging the low slats of the gate.

Catherine laughed. "The worst part of all this is that you probably know exactly what this is and how it goes together. But you don't speak English and I, my equine friend, do not speak Horse."

She moved to the stable gate and stroked the soft nose. The horse whickered again, and Catherine tried an experimental whinny in return. Was it her imagination, or did the horse perk up his ears?

She tried again. Yes, definitely the beast was responding. She whinnied once more and waited, almost expecting to hear a response.

"Ma'am?"

She jumped.

The silhouette of a man stood outlined against the late afternoon sun. Dust from the straw on the barn floor drifted in the hot August air, surrounding him with a slowly moving aura of glistening bits.

She was frozen in place. Her heart had stopped beating entirely, she was sure. He was here to—well, she didn't exactly know what he was here for, but it had to be bad. Men didn't just appear out of nowhere with good intentions.

He moved into the barn, out of the direct sunlight, and walked straight toward her.

The horse nickered, and Catherine stared as the man went directly to the stall, murmuring the name, *Orion,* and holding out an apple he'd taken from his pocket.

The horse bobbed his head up and down in recognition as the man spoke quietly to him.

"You know him?" Catherine wasn't sure how she managed to speak, nor was she sure if she was talking to the horse or to the man.

The man turned, and in the half-light of the dim barn, she could see his face at last.

His was a face shaped by weather—and by laughter.

The lines that were carved in it were premature. He couldn't be much past thirty.

He studied her with eyes as dark as chocolate drops, and then his cheeks crinkled into a smile. "I didn't mean to startle you," he said, extending his hand. "I'm Micah Dunford. I have the next claim over."

Micah Dunford. She knew the name. Her brother had said it before he lapsed back into the deep sleep of a coma.

"I'm glad to meet you." She took the hand and shook it. His grasp was firm and warm, and she could feel the blisters on his palm, evidence of hard work. "Andrew spoke of you."

"You must be Catherine." His fingers gripped hers even tighter. "Andrew talked about you often, about how much he missed you and how much he wished you were here. And now you are. This is wonderful."

She forced her lips into a bad imitation of a smile. "I wish the circumstances were different."

"Of course, of course," he agreed, his words tinged with sadness. "How is Andrew, by the way?"

"When I saw him, he was doing as well as could be expected." She swallowed over the lump that ached in her throat.

"Has he regained consciousness?"

She nodded, fighting the tears that threatened to overwhelm her. "Only for a moment. Just a moment."

The memory of his eyes fluttering open, the way his hand weakly, but distinctly, squeezed her fingers, the single word that tore from his lips, then a too-rapid drop back into that deep sleep—it was too much for her to think about right now.

Micah's forehead furrowed with concern. "I wish him a rapid recovery. Do the doctors have a better picture of his prognosis?"

Catherine blinked back the tight dryness of unshed tears. "They weren't overly worried about the coma. They said it gives his body time to heal. He should be home by late September." She had to clear her throat. "At least that's the hope."

"You know he's in good hands," Micah said softly.

"The doctors at the hospital are the best in the region," she admitted.

"Of course. But I was referring to a more powerful healer."

Catherine stared at him. "There's someone better?" She pulled on his sleeve urgently. "Tell me who he is so I can send him to Andrew!"

"He's already with Him." Micah removed her hand from his arm and grasped it tightly. "I mean God."

"Well, of course." Catherine pulled her hand away, trying to push away the sense of betrayal. "I thought you meant a doctor. That kind of healer."

"God is the Worker of miracles." Micah's dark eyes held hers intently.

"Andrew doesn't need a miracle," she said defiantly. "He just needs sleep."

"Don't you believe?" he asked. "I know Andrew does."

"Of course I believe." She was ready to end this conversation. "My whole family believes. We know who made us, who made this world."

"Do you trust Him?"

Catherine paused. Did she? Resolutely, she shook away the nagging thought. "Naturally." Her answer was brisk and no-nonsense, suppressing the doubt that rose in her chest like bile. "I pray to Him that He will heal Andrew."

Micah nodded as the dust motes danced around his head like an angel's blessing. "I pray that, too."

He touched the pile of harness gear with the booted toe of his foot. "This is Andrew's equipment," he said almost absently. "It's somewhat of a mess right now because we were sorting through it together. We were—"

"I can do it." She moved closer to the tangled pile almost possessively. "It's my responsibility now. Until Andrew comes home and takes over, I'll see to the care of this claim."

Micah tilted his head and studied her. "I'm glad to help. Andrew and I were going to work together anyway."

"It's my responsibility," she repeated. "I'll do it myself."

He lifted an oddly shaped iron bar with his toe and let it drop back into place. "You know how to set this up?" he asked, so quietly that it seemed to Catherine that he was talking to himself.

"I don't, but I can figure it out."

She felt tiny in the barn, overshadowed by the giant horse and the giant man who stood beside her, a half-smile on his face. "Well, I'd best be getting back to my place," he said at last. "I have some things in my barn I need to tend to."

Micah pulled his cap back onto his head and, with a jaunty wave, vanished from the barn.

Catherine watched him walk away, a dark silhouette against the setting sun.

So that was Micah Dunford.

⁓

From the small wooden box on the table, she took out the sampler she had begun stitching during the train trip from Massachusetts. The challenge of the pattern and the clean rhythm of the needle sliding through the cloth calmed her nervous fingers. . .and her equally nervous mind.

She picked up the scrap of material that had been folded and refolded many times in the past week. Smoothing it out on her knees, she could begin to make out the beginning letters of the verse: " 'Be not afraid, only believe.' Mark 5:36."

She picked up her needle and, as she had done so many times, concentrated as the even flow of the thin silver wove in and out of the cloth. Then, she switched to a spring-green strand and began to form yet another letter.

"Be not afraid."

She'd chosen the verse at random. No, that wasn't

true. She'd chosen it because it had reminded her of Andrew. She'd heard him recite the verse often enough.

"Be not afraid."

For years she had lived in his reflected glory, a pale shadow of a girl; too shy to speak, yet always adoring the older brother who had raised her when influenza claimed their parents.

And now she had the chance to repay him for all he'd done. She had to do the job herself. She owed her brother a debt of honor.

But a dreadful debt. If only Andrew had stayed in Massachusetts, he would still be safe. The wanderlust in him, that enthusiastic embracing of the challenges of life, had called him out here to this dreadful land, where a simple fall off a wagon had put him in the deathlike sleep of a coma.

Dakota Territory. Even the name sounded cold and forbidding.

She glanced out the window as the last bits of daylight left the tiny house. She would have to light the lamp soon.

Yet, on the seemingly endless, infinite horizon, a glorious array spread over the land. The sky burst into brilliant pinks and purples and oranges and reds, turning the amber fields a fiery crimson.

Catherine's breath caught in her throat. She'd never seen such a sunset.

Still, even a magnificent sunset could not draw her to this place. Nothing, absolutely nothing would convince her to stay in Dakota once Andrew was healthy again.

Given the first chance, she'd talk him into coming back to Massachusetts with her, back to a life that was normal and predictable, where his livelihood didn't depend upon a tangled pile of leather and metal.

Well, all this musing would do nothing but make her crazy. She rose and stood on her tiptoes to take a lamp from the shelf.

A piece of paper fluttered down, and she picked it up curiously.

It was a letter to her in Andrew's handwriting, dated the day of his accident. Eagerly she scanned the page, relishing the sound of his written voice as he relayed the daily workings of the claim.

The words at the end brought her up short.

"I want you to come out here," he'd written. "I have already told you about Micah Dunford, and the more I see of him, the more impressed I am. I want you to be happy, Catherine. I want to see you with children around you. I want to see you smiling at your husband as he comes home from the fields."

Her eyes clouded with tears as she read. "Micah is a safe man. A kind man, a good man, a Christian man. He is the kind of man you should love. Give this some thought, Catherine. Pray about it. I hope you do not think me too forward to suggest this so boldly, but I have prayed about how to broach the subject, and I feel that God would want me to say my piece straightforward."

Her breath caught at the next words. "I have spoken

to him about all this and he says that he has prayed for a helpmeet to join him here. Catherine, might it be—" And the letter ended.

She sat down in the chair, the unlit lamp beside her. Micah thought she was the answer to his prayer?

"Oh, my," she said aloud. "Oh, my."

Across the summer prairie, a beam of light stretched from an open window and spilled onto the ground beyond the small house. The glow from the single lamp conquered the surrounding darkness, illuminating a man bent over a well-worn book.

He read carefully, sometimes frowning, sometimes smiling.

At last he shut the book and closed his eyes. He missed his prayer partner, but there were some prayers that needed to be private.

"My Father, she is here. I prayed for her and now she is here. I sense that she is not here to answer the need in me, perhaps, but to fill the need in herself. You sent her here for a purpose—a purpose which may be clear to You, but, at the moment, is not clear to me. She is special, Lord. This woman is truly special."

Chapter 2

The shadows fell around Catherine as she sat in the chair, the letter in her hand and the still-unlit lamp at her side. She knew she should rise and place a match's flame to the wick and bring the darkness into light, but she could not.

Marriage!

Throughout her childhood, she had dreamed of having a husband and a child of her own, but, so far, she had experienced only the vaguest flickerings of interest from the young men around her.

And the mirror reminded her daily, she wasn't getting any younger. At this stage, she'd pretty much resigned herself to a lifetime of being alone.

Marriage!

There was, at the word, a stirring of that young girl, so many years ago, who had rocked her doll under the careful eye of her brother, and who had dreamed of someday holding a real-life baby while her husband gazed at her.

A baby is still a possibility, she reminded herself practically, *but not without a husband.* That much she did know.

Her fingers traced the words on Andrew's letter. The idea that her brother wanted her married and settled wasn't all that odd. He'd always taken his responsibility quite seriously. It was only natural that he'd want to see her happily wedded.

No, the strange part was that Andrew had chosen Micah.

Clearly there's a dearth of eligible bachelors on the prairie, she told herself.

But even so, the image of Micah's deep brown eyes, as soft as warmed chocolate, the laugh lines etched much too early in his face, the open concern for her brother's welfare—all these were signs that Andrew was right in his assessment of Micah.

Catherine laughed aloud. Yes, she knew so much about this man. She'd talked to him for all of five minutes and had him well summed up.

She laid the letter on the table beside her chair and stood up. Dusk had deepened into absolute night, and she found the matches only with the aid of the starlight that flooded through the undraped window.

She paused before striking the match and gazed out the window. The prairie glowed with the light of the stars and the full moon overhead. As far as she could see, the nighttime prairie stretched ahead of her. A vast expanse of dark land-sea, nearly ripened wheat nodding in waves before the wind that rippled the top-heavy stalks.

But this was an empty land. As far as her eyes could see, the only visible structures were the small house and barn on Andrew's claim—and whatever buildings Micah had on his.

Across the shadowy distance, a light twinkled, and she wondered if it might not be Micah's claim. She had no idea how far away he lived. All she knew was that Andrew had mentioned that Micah's place was "near," but here on the prairie, "near" seemed a relative term. Nothing was near.

Catherine turned from the window and lit the lamp at last. The light poured into the room, making it seem like a haven against the darkness that pressed against the outer walls.

She picked up the embroidery that she'd laid aside.

The piece was destined to be a welcome-home gift for Andrew. She'd worked on it all the way from Massachusetts, taking solace from the even flash of the silver needle through the textured Hardanger cloth. Each slice of the needle through the cloth had marked her progress one stitch closer to Andrew and then, after realizing that, one stitch closer to Dakota.

The rhythm of the cross-stitch had echoed the pulse of the train's wheels on the rails, and now, as she began her stitching again, she could almost feel the subtle swaying of the train car as it had lumbered through the forests and into the plains.

The piece, when finished, would be a surprise for her brother. It was meant for Andrew, but she recognized that she was also making it for herself. Always shy and tending to hide behind Andrew's exuberant exterior, the verse was selected for her as well as for him. "Be not afraid, only believe."

The task ahead of her was great.

She'd realized that fact as soon as she'd seen the tangle of implements on the barn floor. A part of her wanted to run away from this spot and go back to her safe life in Massachusetts.

Andrew would understand. He had always understood. He hadn't expected much of his timid little sister. But this time, she mustn't let him down.

This was her chance to prove to him—and to herself—that she could do something besides her usual day-to-day activities in Massachusetts at the dressmaker's. She had insulated herself from challenge, but that was going to change. Starting with the mess on the floor of the barn.

She laid the embroidery aside and stood up resolutely. She would go to the barn and take another look at the heap of leather straps and metal pieces and see if she couldn't at least sort through them a bit.

She wrapped her shawl around her shoulders. There was a hint of rain in the thick August night air.

Then, with the lantern in hand, she made her way to the barn.

Barn swallows swooped at her head, and she swatted

them away. They were vehemently protecting their nests, she knew, but they were such a bother.

The barn seemed cavernous at night. Her lamp's light barely pierced the dark corners.

Orion whinnied a soft greeting from his stall and tossed his head at her.

She'd forgotten to bring him a snack, but she noticed an apple on the shelf by the door. She hadn't put it there. It must be something Micah had left.

She fed it to the horse, trying not to cringe as the big horse's mouth opened and closed around the apple she held in her fingers.

But he was gentle and good, this horse, and didn't even nip her as he took the apple from her.

She rubbed his soft nose and spoke to him before turning to the business at hand: sorting out the knotted bindings and their associated metal pieces.

She nudged the pile with her toe and considered her next step. *What I need to do,* she decided, *is untangle it.* She knelt beside the pile and began the tedious task of separating it into smaller parts.

She was actually beginning to enjoy the chore. *This feels like real progress,* she decided as she laid one entire section aside neatly. Once she got this figured out, the rest would be no problem at all.

"Show yourself!"

The words from the entrance to the barn brought her to her feet quickly. Her heart pounded its way into her throat, and she snatched the lantern and held it high so she could see who the intruder was.

It was Micah, and she could see from his face that he was as terrified as she was.

They both spoke at once, their words falling over the other's.

"You scared me to death!"

"I thought you were a robber!"

"Don't *ever* do that again!"

"Don't *you* ever do that again!"

"You scared the wits out of me!"

"Me? You!"

They stared at each other and then broke into the laughter that comes with relief.

"I thought you were someone breaking into Andrew's barn," Micah said.

"And I—well, I don't know what I thought, if I thought at all. I was suddenly overcome with an awful panic." She paused as a dreadful realization struck home. She was quite alone in that small house, with nothing but the vast prairie around her.

As if he could read her thoughts, Micah smiled gently but seriously. The lamplight cast golden sparks in his deep brown eyes. "There is a natural cause for worry, Catherine. The prairie has dangers of its own, and there are certainly those who would take advantage of anyone here alone."

Her fear must have shown in her face, because his look deepened. "You are not alone, though, not really. Don't forget that there is a Creator who watches over you every minute."

"Yes, of course. But the Creator who made me also made the wolf."

He nodded. "You do have a gun?"

The last was more a question than a statement.

"Yes, I suppose I do." Catherine realized that he was referring to the rifle hung over a window in the house.

"Do you know how to use it?"

"If need be," she hedged. In fact, she had never once found such a need. There was some way to put bullets in it, and, yes, pull the trigger. That much she knew. It wasn't enough, but she was absolutely not going to experiment to find out how to shoot a gun.

Micah nodded. "I see. Well, if you don't mind, I will stop by and check on you each night."

She could feel her chin rising defiantly. "You don't have to check on me."

"It's no problem. I check on my stock—the cattle, the horses, and the pigs—anyway, and I'll simply add you to the list."

"Your *stock?* I'm not some kind of farm animal, sir!" She realized too late that he was teasing her.

He was laughing as he turned to leave. "You know, Miss Cooper, I think you're going to be an interesting neighbor. I never guessed that Andrew had such a delightful sister."

And, as quickly as he had filled the barn with life and warmth, he was gone.

She crossed her arms over her chest and shivered

involuntarily, despite the heavy summer heat. The claim seemed so empty without his shielding presence.

The words from Andrew's unmailed letter came back to her. "Micah is a safe man. A kind man, a good man, a Christian man." Andrew had trusted him, and so should she. At this stage, unsure as she was on the frontier, she needed to rely on him for certain things.

As she left the barn, she stumbled over the edge of the harvesting gear.

She would *not* rely on him to save Andrew's claim. That was her duty, her self-assigned task. If she could do that, it would settle, once and for all, the debt she felt toward her brother.

She hurried across the short distance between the barn and the house, grateful for the sanctuary of the small house at last.

Her thoughts still centered on Micah, and at the core of them all was the fact that she liked having him near her. He made her feel safe and confident and welcome.

He was all those things Andrew had said.

But as she was getting ready to blow out the lamp and retire for the night, the next sentence in her brother's letter leaped into her mind.

"He is the kind of man you should love."

⌒∿

The night wrapped the prairie in a blanket of black, illuminated only by starlight.

The man was exhausted, but for him, prayer was as necessary as sleep. He took the time to talk to his Lord.

He smiled as he prayed. "You invented laughter, Lord, and You know I've needed some in my life lately. She has a certain way of smiling that makes my heart laugh. You are blessing me in a strange way, Lord."

Chapter 3

"Be not afraid,
only believe."
Mark 5:36

Catherine awoke the next morning tired and out of sorts, feeling as if she'd tossed and turned all night long—but then again, that was precisely what she had done. Images of Micah had flown in and out of her mind like the swallows that swooped at her whenever she entered the barn, relentlessly diving and plunging at her head.

If only I hadn't found Andrew's letter, she told herself as she splashed cold water on her face, *things would be fine.* Micah would simply be a neighbor, a friend of her brother. She would never have studied those tiny laugh lines that the sun had etched around his eyes. Nor would she have noticed those golden glints that sparkled in his deep brown eyes. And she certainly never would have paid any attention to the way her heart seemed to smile when she saw him.

I'm probably lonely, she decided as she dried off her face. What she needed to do was to get her mind off this entire situation by getting to work.

And there was plenty of work to do. The garden needed quite a bit of work. It had become overgrown and, according to her quick survey, quite a feast for the rabbits.

She was no gardener, but she could do some harvesting of the yellow squash that the rabbits had left alone, and the carrots, which were safely underground. She tried to drive down the voice that challenged her to know a ripe squash from an unripe one. Hadn't she purchased squash in the market just two weeks ago?

Squash that tasted dry and awful, the little voice persisted in her ear.

She dismissed the nagging words with the reminder that she would be the one to eat the food, and if it were unripe or overripe, she would not find it much different than that which she bought in the city.

The air was hot and clear as she shrugged into her lightest dress. She planned to finish the garden today, then move toward harvesting the fields. They looked quite ripe to her, but the tiny voice roared: *You don't know a head of wheat from a thistle seed!* The nagging thought was only a slight exaggeration.

She should probably talk to Micah a bit and learn everything he could tell her about harvesting.

She realized she was smiling and tried to stop.

But there was something—something very special about Micah Dunford.

The garden was an untamed tangle of weeds and vegetables, but she realized that her task ahead was not as major as she'd feared. The squash were recognizable by the fortunate fact that they grew above ground. All she had to do was pick the familiar shapes. The carrots, although underground, had distinguishing leafy tops that clearly identified them. The carrots she'd purchased in Massachusetts came attached to the same feathery greens.

As she moved through the garden, lifting a mass of leaves here and pulling a recalcitrant root there, she let her mind drift to the strange circumstances that had brought her here, to the strange land that was the Dakota Territory.

She'd almost pushed the worry about Andrew out of her mind, afraid of coming too close to it. The thought of losing him was so incredibly painful that even the briefest flicker of that image pressed on her soul with an unimaginable anguish.

It was easier to focus on other things, like the sampler she was stitching, or the puzzle of the harvesting equipment in the barn, or the incredible sweetness of Micah's smile.

A sharp prick brought her back to reality. She looked down and realized that she had grasped a thistle rather than a carrot top. Her fingers and palms were filled with the nearly invisible spikes.

The stinging was intense, and before she could stop herself, she stuck her fingers in her mouth, trying to pull out the tiny needles with her teeth.

"Were you planning on serving that tonight?" Micah

asked as he came up behind her. He moved the offending plant off the pile of freshly pulled carrots and threw it into the rubbish heap. "We'll burn that later. It's the only way to get rid of those nasty things. In the meantime, let me see your hands."

He took hold of her hands, and with a skillful gentleness that surprised her, studied the situation. "Amazing. You used both hands, too. What a mess. Let's move into the full sunshine and I'll see what I can do."

One by one, he took out the thistle's spikes, and as he did, Catherine had the chance to study him. How old was he? He couldn't be much past thirty, but the sun had done its aging on him. He seemed so much a part of the Dakota Territory, every bit the image of the hearty homesteader; still, there were other parts of him that she wanted to tap.

Of course, she'd known him for only a day. There were all sorts of hidden possibilities. Just because her brother had suggested that he might be her husband. . .

He looked at her suddenly, and she had the horrible thought that she must have said something or made a sound. But he smiled. "All through."

He stood up and wiped his hands on his shirt. "Your hands might sting a bit tonight, but other than that, there shouldn't be any lasting effects."

"Good, because I have some work to do. I'd like to finish the garden today."

He glanced at the two piles she'd made on the ground, one of vegetables and the other of weeds, and then at the garden plot. "Looks like you've already finished the garden."

From the way he said it, the laughter just under the surface of his words, she knew that she'd bungled the task. Perhaps not totally—that much was obvious from the pile that included the carrots—but in her weeded heap must be some plants that were edible.

She shrugged. Whatever they were, she probably didn't want to eat them. If she couldn't see them, they couldn't be worth much, except for the carrots.

"Dig under here and you'll probably find potatoes." Micah pointed to one of the sections that she'd stripped the greenery from. "That was very clever of you to clear the tops so digging would be easier."

Catherine tried to act as if that had, indeed, been her plan, but she knew—and he knew—that she'd had no idea that beneath those viny plants grew potatoes.

"I came over here, actually, for another reason," Micah said, suddenly changing the subject. "When do you want to start bringing in the wheat?"

"I was going to put the equipment together this afternoon." She was sure she saw the corner of his mouth twitch, as if he were trying to suppress a smile. She drew herself up straighter. "I can do this myself, you know."

"I don't doubt that for a moment, but you should be aware that Dakotans, well, we watch out for each other. It may not look like the neighborhoods that you're used to, but on the prairie, that's exactly what it is—a neighborhood. And we help out when we can, even when we can't. We've got to. That's the way we survive."

Catherine looked out over the prairie, now so rich with unharvested wheat, but in her mind, she pictured the land covered over with snow. Instead of undulating in subtle waves, almost as if they were breathing, the fields of wheat would too soon transform to fields of snow. A frozen paradise? Hardly.

Whatever feelings for Micah that might have been budding in her withered and died. He was a man committed to life in the Dakota Territory, and she wanted nothing more than to see Andrew healthy and safe—away from this land that had injured him.

The only way she could see to do that was to get the crop in, sold, then use the money to pay the doctors and buy them both train tickets bound for Massachusetts.

"I'm sure that's true," she told him, amazed at the backbone she suddenly felt, "but I have a commitment here to take care of this myself. I can do it." She swallowed. "I have to do it."

He moved a bit closer to her, and she realized that he was not angry at her words. His true concern radiated from him. "Please remember that I am always ready to help you. If there is anything at all that I can do, I'm just over there." He pointed at a spot on the distant horizon and, in spite of herself, Catherine laughed.

"Just over there? So if I need a cup of sugar, I can just stop in." She shook her head. "This place is very strange. My next-door neighbor is more than a mile away."

"Speaking of borrowing a cup of sugar, there is one thing I do need to get from you. Andrew had ordered a hoe blade that's due to come in, and since I'm going into Fargo anyway, I can pick it up if it's there. I'll need his receipt, though."

"You're welcome to come in," she said, "although I have no idea where it might be."

He smiled, his even, white teeth flashing in the sunlight. "I know exactly where he kept them. Andrew stuck everything of importance in his Bible."

As they entered the house, Micah looked around admiringly. "Andrew put a lot into this house. He didn't have anyone special yet—he said he was waiting to get established before he'd find himself a wife—but he did say that he wanted to bring his wife home to a good house, one that would make them both proud."

"What is your house like?" she asked, and as soon as the words were out of her mouth, she realized how they must sound. Her face flooded with warmth.

But he didn't seem to notice. "It's about the same size as this one, but not quite as finished. I still have a board floor and everything needs paint."

He reached for the Bible. "Andrew always kept this in the same place." He ran his hand over the leather cover. "Sometimes we'd sit in the summer sunshine, having worked in the fields all day, and we'd try to outdo each other in a Bible verse game. Andrew would quote a verse, and I'd have to identify it, or at least give its context. And then it'd be my turn. I hardly ever beat him at it."

"Just like men," Catherine said, blinking back the tears at the image of her brother healthy and whole. "Always competitive, even with the Bible!"

Micah shrugged. "The game helped us learn the Word. Out here, occasionally a circuit-rider minister might come through, but pretty much we're on our own for religious education. So, we do the best we can."

He picked up the sampler she had laid aside. " 'Be not afraid, only believe.' That's Andrew's favorite verse. He said it was what sustained him."

Micah looked away, and Catherine saw that he was blinking rapidly. *He's crying!*

Of course. Why hadn't she realized it before? They were best friends, Andrew and Micah. Now Micah was alone, just as she was.

Her heart softened, and she reached to touch his arm in reassurance.

As she did, Micah turned and a piece of paper fluttered out of the Bible he held. He leaned over to pick it up. "This must be the receipt—" he began, but Catherine noticed the handwriting and snatched it away from him.

It was the letter from Andrew, the one in which he asked Catherine to consider Micah as a husband.

Had he seen the words? His expression hadn't changed, so he must not have.

She took the Bible from him and, trying to cover her confusion, leafed through it until she found the receipt.

"Remember, if you ever need help, let me know. I'll be over every day to check on things here," he said as he took the paper from her. He touched the Bible she held. "And don't forget the Friend. You are never alone here."

He left, and she sank into the chair with a sigh of relief.

She liked Micah—liked him quite a bit—but she kept seeing him as a potential husband, thanks to Andrew's letter.

Thankfully, he hadn't read her brother's letter. What would he think if—

She sat up straight. She was so dumb sometimes. Of course he knew. The letter said he'd discussed it with Andrew.

All along, he'd known.

After seeing her, was that still his intention?

Her heart answered with a fervent wish that surprised her: *yes*.

⁂

His mind finally closed around the bit of information he'd been pushing away: the letter from Andrew in the Bible. He hadn't read it—the words weren't meant for him—but he wondered what it said. The way she had snatched the page away made him wonder if Andrew had mentioned their plan to her.

It wasn't something he was proud of. In fact, he was downright ashamed. He seemed no better than those desperate men who got mail-order brides to live with them out here.

She deserved better. Much better.

"Dearest Father, take away that thought from me and let me start fresh with Catherine. I see in her everything I have wanted in a wife, but my affection grows too soon. Help me guard my words, guard my eyes, guard my thoughts. She is a woman I could love. . . ."

Chapter 4

"Be not afraid, only believe."
Mark 5:36

What she needed to do was quit mooning around like she was a young girl. It was pointless, and besides, she had work to do.

Resolutely, Catherine strode out to the barn, prepared to do battle with the equipment that still lay in a huddle on the packed-earth floor.

The straps and metal bits seemed to have intertwined themselves even more since her last visit here. She sighed and dropped to a sitting position to begin the laborious process of untangling them.

It was a nearly automatic process, wrapping this strap around that, moving the darkened silver of the metal loops here, pulling the harness pieces free.

There was something familiar about it, and at last Catherine understood.

The motion mirrored that of her sewing, the same in and out, over and through, of her needle flashing through the cloth. And in the end, both efforts would be pleasing to her brother.

Knowing that, she approached her task at hand with renewed enthusiasm, taking pleasure from the rhythmic unweaving of the snarled pile.

At last, she laid the final leather strip into place and leaned back with satisfaction. An immediate pain in the small of her back ran up her spine and reminded her that she had been sitting in one position entirely too long.

Sunset had begun to fall without her even realizing it. Long shadows cast the barn into pools of scattered darkness. She stood up slowly and painfully as the kinks worked themselves out of her back and hobbled back into the house.

What she needed was a good cup of tea and a soak in a warm bath. She built up the fire and put two large kettles on to heat.

She glanced longingly at her embroidery. A part of her wanted to pick it up and stitch some more, but the ache in her arms stopped her. And whenever she shut her eyes, even for a moment, all she saw was a hodge-podge of straps, and the image swam in front of her eyes as she ran her fingers over the silky floss.

Catherine shuddered. The dye on the leather had stained her fingertips black. She wouldn't be able to embroider anyway. Not without the risk of getting the cloth and thread stained.

It was a pity, but her important duty was to the harvest—and to her brother.

⁓

Orion whinnied and shook his head. The horse's mane

shimmered in the early morning light. Someone—Micah, probably—had been here grooming Orion, she realized guiltily. She'd basically been ignoring the beast, except for feeding him and turning him loose in the enclosed paddock area for some exercise.

"You're a good boy," she cooed, stroking the gray velvet nose. When he had calmed down, she led him from the stall into the bright sunshine outside.

Orion stamped his feet nervously as she approached him with the first bit of equipment that she felt sure was the harness, but the horse let her slip the straps onto his massive neck and body.

She stood back, inordinately pleased at how well this initial step had gone.

But the rest was not nearly as easy. Two hours later, sweaty and frustrated, she was unbuckling Orion from the harness when Micah rode up.

She would have felt considerably better if he hadn't burst into laughter at what she had done.

He leaped off his horse and raced to Orion. As he rearranged the system of straps, buckles, and rings, he spoke to the horse softly. Catherine was sure she heard her name mentioned repeatedly as he chuckled occasionally in the horse's ear.

What she had unsuccessfully struggled to do, for the better part of the morning, he did easily in little more than a matter of minutes.

As he hooked up the equipment to the harness, he told her the purpose of each part.

"And then you have to hook it up to the binder," he finished.

"The binder. All right. It's in here, right?" She rummaged through the odd bits that were left after she'd assembled the harness.

He was trying not to laugh. She could see that.

"No," he answered slowly, and he rubbed his hand over his mouth in a futile attempt to hide his smile. "Come with me."

He led her into the barn. "It's back here."

She hadn't noticed the contraption before, mainly because she had not explored the shadowed corners of the huge barn, but she felt dense and stupid not to have noticed it.

It was a big contraption, larger than she'd ever expected. It looked somewhat like a paddle wheel, but with thinner blades.

Her mind spun with the words as he tried to explain the process. "It'll gather the grain into bundles, and then we'll put those bundles together into shocks, and then it'll all go through a threshing machine."

She nodded, but it didn't make any sense.

"You really do need more than one horse for this," he warned. "Usually, people use four horses, but Andrew and I scaled this down to make it work with ours. We'd planned for both of our horses to pull the binder."

If she had to stand in place of one of the horses and pull the plow herself, she would. She would not accept anyone's help.

"Let me show you how this works," he said, leading Orion to the edge of the field.

He led Orion, and she wondered if he was pulling the binder, too, to lighten the load.

It looked so easy as she watched them, man and horse, working together to harvest the wheat. They moved as one, both used to the rhythm of the field-work. There would be no problem for her to finish this herself, and she told him so.

For a moment, Micah looked at her, studying her face. "You really want to do this—" he motioned toward the vast field "—all by yourself?"

"Yes, yes," she said impatiently, anxious to get on with the task while she still had the image of how it worked in her mind.

He held the reins, as if weighing something in his mind, and at last he nodded and handed them to her.

"I'll be in my own fields today," he said, "but don't hesitate to come over if you'd like some help."

"I. . .don't. . .want. . .any. . .help," she said with deliberate slowness. "Now go and tend to your own work. I'll be fine here. Come along, Orion."

And without a further look backward, she stepped into the field and began the harvest on her own.

Catherine sat in the middle of the downed wheat and buried her face in her hands. All around her was the day's work, and the result was nothing more than total destruction.

The job had looked so easy when Micah had done it. He had simply walked through the field, leading Orion, and the wheat had fallen neatly.

And then he'd said something about a machine that would finish the work.

Or that's what she thought he'd said.

She raised her head and looked around her. The wheat was strewn here and there. The kernels had already fallen off most of it, and the blackbirds had quickly discovered what a delightful treat she'd provided for them.

No machine invented by man could come through here and repair the damage she'd done. She had ruined this section entirely.

Orion stamped his hooves impatiently, and she got to her feet. "I know, I know," she told the horse, "I don't quite have the touch yet."

The awful truth was that she didn't have the touch at all. Orion had been nervous throughout her attempts to harvest the wheat, clearly recognizing her inexperience.

The horse hadn't been that way with Micah, she thought somewhat grumpily.

She unhooked Orion from the equipment, leaving it lying in the field, and walked him back to the barn, ignoring the wide swaths of clumsily mowed wheat that lay behind her like accusatory wounds on her brother's land.

After getting Orion cleaned up and fed, she trudged back into the house and cleaned and fed herself.

There was more to this harvest thing than she'd allowed herself to admit. Why had the plow worked so well for Micah and not for her?

She put her head back and shut her eyes. She visualized the equipment, pictured it working. And then, she knew what she had done wrong.

Quickly, she jumped up and ran to the fields through the gathering darkness. Mosquitoes surrounded her like a biting cloud, but she ignored them.

She leaned over and examined the rig where it lay on the ground. And then, she stood up with a sigh of satisfaction. She'd been right. A piece had come unhooked.

With a lighter heart, she walked back to the small house. Things were looking better already.

The next evening, Catherine looked over a somewhat erratically harvested section of the field. It was uneven, to be sure, but the work was done.

And in that she felt a measure of satisfaction that was almost overwhelming in its intensity.

The next day she worked, and the next, and the next, and each day the rhythm got easier, and she and Orion wove through the field with the same cadence of her silver needle shooting through the cloth on the sampler.

The rhythm is all the same, she thought. She simply had to tackle the task and do it to the best of her ability. All along, she had been embroidering it: "Only believe."

The field, when harvested, might not look as neat and tidy as Micah's undoubtedly did, but to her it was quickly becoming a thing of beauty, as sure as her colorful sampler inside.

Catherine smiled at the full moon that shone over the decimated part of the field. "I can do this," she said aloud. "I really can do it."

❧

The sun had just come up on the prairie. *The early morning walk will do me good*, he told himself. The long pace after the short start-stop rhythm of the early harvest was good exercise for a man.

He didn't have as much time as he would have liked to come by and check on her progress, so if his morning walk took him by her fields, all the better.

It had been difficult, just watching and not being able to help as she tried repeatedly to get the binder to work.

But she had accomplished the feat.

He felt as proud as if he'd done it himself.

Lord, every day is a delight with You. You are the sun on the fields, the rain from the heavens, the nourishment of the soil. May this harvest and all who work it be a blessing to You.

Chapter 5

"Be not afraid,
only believe."
Mark 5:36

She could hear his horse's hooves on the ground even before she saw him. Sound carried with an astonishing intensity on the prairie.

Something was driving him onward. He'd never ridden that fast or that furious.

His horse had barely stopped before Micah swung his legs over the saddle and leaped off in a seamless dismount.

In his hand he held a piece of paper.

"This. . .came. . . ." He was clearly winded.

She took the note from him without wiping the rich valley soil from her hands. It was a telegram.

Her eyes scanned it quickly. There were only a few words, but they were powerful ones.

"Andrew is—?"

Micah shook his head. "He's alive, but his condition is worsening, Catherine. They're. . .they're concerned."

"Concerned?" She realized too late that she was shouting. "I'm sorry. I didn't mean to yell at you. But he's going to be all right, isn't he?"

She wanted to see him smile. She wanted to hear his laugh as he told her it was all a joke. But the look on his face told her that this was all grimly real.

She looked again at the telegram. The words swam in front of her. Something about swelling in his brain. . . .

"I have to go to St. Paul," she said. "I have to see him."

"I don't think they'll let you," he responded gently. "He needs absolute quiet right now. He's in a deep coma and even if he could move, he shouldn't. The brain does swell from trauma, and—"

"How do you know all this? Are you a prairie doctor?" she asked.

He shook his head. "Son of a doctor. Until he retired, my father practiced at St. Elizabeth's, the hospital where Andrew is."

"Why did the message come to you rather than to me?" she asked.

"I didn't know that you were coming. I could only hope that you were. So I used my name as the contact person. I got this wire because I went into Fargo to pick up the harness bit that your brother ordered."

Catherine looked at the wire. It was dated four days earlier. "Look at this! By now, he could be d—" She couldn't bring herself to say the word.

"He's not dead. I sent a follow-up wire and waited for the response. It said simply, 'No change.' I did ask that if—*when*—Andrew awakens, that he's told you are near. We can be there in a day, if we ride the horses hard."

She ran her hand across her forehead, aware that she was probably wiping a streak of dirt across her sweat-soaked forehead but not caring. "Let's go now."

"We can't. We couldn't do anything anyway. We can best serve Andrew by bringing in his crop. Knowing that his crop is safe will speed him to recovery more than anything when he comes out of the coma."

He moved toward her. "Let me help you, Catherine."

She shook her head. "No. This is something I have to do myself. And, right now, Micah—" Her voice faltered and she paused before continuing. "Right now, I think I need to be by myself."

He nodded. "I understand. If it's all right with you, I'll stop back by tonight to see if there's anything you need."

She looked at him sadly. "The only thing I need is my brother with me, whole again."

"Have you taken this to the Lord?" he asked.

Catherine shook her head mutely.

"He made the blind see and the deaf hear," Micah said. "You might ask Him to help Andrew."

She could only nod, numbly, before running into the house.

The tears would not come. She would not allow that. That would be a sign of weakness, and she could not permit herself even a moment of weakness.

Catherine paced the perimeter of the small house, picking up this and studying that.

This was Andrew's, all Andrew's. She was the care-taker, custodian of everything he owned.

The house was small, but it was more than most people had on the prairie. She knew that. If the crop didn't come in, if the money from it weren't realized, everything would be lost. The house, which she was sure had been built with borrowed money, would go back to the bank. The land would go back to the government.

And Andrew would come back to her.

How long she stood in that spot, she had no idea. Micah must have taken Orion in, curried him, and fed him, because she heard his soft whinny from the barn in response to the early evening hoot of an owl.

The August days here in Dakota were long, providing an astonishing number of hours of daylight. But twilight, when its time did arrive, fell quickly on the summer prairie, and darkness raced across the flat land.

She moved to light the lamp and as she did, her glance fell upon the sampler, long forgotten as she'd focused on bringing in the harvest.

She picked it up and, after moving the lamp closer to her elbow, began the stitching again.

"Be not afraid, only believe."

Her needle moved in and out of the cloth, pulling this time an orchid thread the same hue as the last traces of the prairie sunset.

I'll finish this one word, she told herself, *and then I'll lay down and try to sleep.* She needed sleep to finish the harvest. And Micah was right—having the harvest done would be a powerful medicine for her brother.

Over and down, across and up. Over and down, across and up. The words her grandmother had taught her so long ago came back to her. They were the pattern of cross-stitch.

The orchid was a beautiful color in the skein, but it paled as a single thread on the off-white background. But, she reminded herself, other colors would come in that would work together. No one would even notice that the orchid thread was there. Instead, there would be a glorious display of purples and golds and greens, all blending together as completely as a sunset.

There. She had finished the first part of the word. Andrew would be proud of her work.

She buried her face in the sampler. Andrew. She wanted him to live more than anything. He had to live. He simply had to.

She could not cry, especially into the sampler. She smoothed it over her knee, forcing herself to check the stitching on the letters.

The pale thread caught the lamplight and seemed to make the word she'd just stitched glow: "Believe."

Believe? In what? That he would live?

Or that he would die?

She couldn't bear the thought. She arose, snatched her shawl from the post by the door, and walked outside.

Autumn was coming on the wind. She could smell it. She could hear it. The sharp edge of the yet-warm wind whipped her skirt around her ankles. Winter would soon follow, carried on the crisp promise of icy crystals.

The harvest couldn't wait. No matter what was happening with Andrew in St. Paul, she had to bring in the crops.

She walked out into the partially harvested field, remembering her early flippancy about getting the crop in. She had stood here, at the edge of this very field, and asked herself, "How hard can it be?"

Now she knew.

The night wind carried the sound of hoofbeats. Micah was coming. She recognized his approaching figure in the bright moonlight.

He was at her side quickly. "Are you all right?"

She nodded. "It's so warm and yet, I can't stop shivering."

"Winter will be here before we know it," he said, and she glanced at him in surprise.

"How odd. I was just thinking about that," she said.

"You're becoming one of us." His dark eyes twinkled.

"One of you? In what way?"

"A farmer is always thinking about the weather."

She laughed, grateful to have her thoughts shifted away from her troubles. "I don't think that I will ever be a farmer."

"A farmer's wife, perhaps?"

She whirled to face him. "Excuse me?"

"I wondered if you'd be a farmer's wife someday." His voice was bland.

"Why do you ask?" Her voice sounded shaky and high-pitched to her ears.

"I simply asked to ask, that's all."

Her heart was racing as fast as the prairie wind. "Then I will answer to answer. I will marry the man I love, and if he is a greengrocer, then I am a greengrocer's wife. If he is a carpenter, then I am a carpenter's wife. And if he is a farmer, then I am a farmer's wife."

He didn't respond, and Catherine knew she may have said exactly the wrong thing, but she didn't know what else she could have said.

She took a deep breath. "I think I will go inside now. I would like an early start tomorrow."

He caught her arm as she turned to leave. "Catherine, would you do me a favor?"

"What?" she responded numbly.

He probably wanted to borrow a tool or perhaps have her mend a torn seam in his jacket. This was an odd time to make such a request.

But she was not ready for his response.

"Pray with me."

A thousand questions collided and shoved their way around her bruised and battered heart. Pray to God? Why? What had God done for Andrew? Injured him and then put him in a faraway hospital to die?

Why should she pray to this God who did such terrible things to good people? Andrew hadn't deserved this fate. He was a man who loved his Lord, who tithed not only his money but his time in devotion.

It seemed to Catherine that God had allowed someone as caring and kind and gentle as Andrew to suffer.

She wasn't inclined to offer Him her prayers.

But Andrew would be so inclined if the situation were reversed, she heard her heart say.

Suddenly all her resolve, all her opposition, melted away with a flood of tears.

She opened herself to what was true and real. She could no longer avoid the truth.

The raw wounds on her soul were nothing compared to those of her Lord. Jesus had died for her. He had borne her sins and promised her life eternal.

With a force more powerful than she had imagined possible, she understood about this God that Andrew and Micah worshipped.

The words she had been stitching on cloth were now embroidered onto her heart: "Be not afraid, only believe."

Her worries were His, and He could shoulder them when her endurance was taxed to the limit.

She just had to ask. The solution was that simple.

"I am Yours, God," she said, and with those words of surrender, she became a new being.

Micah's arms were waiting for her, and together they dropped to their knees.

There, in the field amidst half-harvested wheat, with the warmth of summer and the promise of autumn around them, the two offered to God their most fervent prayers for Andrew's healing and recovery.

As the words flowed from their hearts and lips, Catherine felt a release such as she'd never known before. What they said didn't seem to matter as much as what they felt, and the power around them was so strong that she was sure it could be felt in St. Paul.

There was a special warmth in Micah's touch as he helped her to her feet and, although neither said much of consequence before he left, much had indeed been said between them.

God was with them both. And, yes, she could be a farmer's wife.

❧

Both he and his horse were thirsty, and the creek ran clear and cold. He swung off the saddle, and both horse and man drank deeply from the refreshing stream.

The horse was content to graze a bit, so he sat under the lone cottonwood and looked out over his prairie, for that was how he thought of it.

His prairie. It was as if he and the rich soil, the blue sky, the astonishingly white clouds, were all one.

It was good.

It lacked only one thing. Someone to share it with. And now Catherine was here. Was she the one?

His prayer was short: "Lord, am I seeing only what I want, and not what I need?"

Chapter 6

"Be not afraid,
only believe."
Mark 5:36

Nothing seemed to ease Catherine's mind except focusing solely on the harvest. Daily she strained to finish the reaping, always reminding herself to take it slowly and carefully.

The ruined section lay as a mute testimony to her earlier rashness. It looked to her, for all the world, like a bad haircut—stalks left standing here, others leveled to the ground there.

❧

Two weeks later, she stood at the house, her noonday meal in hand, admiring the work she'd done. She could see the improvement in the way the stalks lay neatly, ready for sheaving. That would be the next step.

The news from St. Paul was patchy, at best. Updates had arrived, and the news was not good. Andrew's condition was worsening.

Once the crop was in safely, once the harvest was done, she would go to St. Paul and see him.

It might be her last chance to see him alive.

Stated so baldly, the realization was terrifying, but she'd thought the words often enough to blister over them. She centered on the word "alive" rather than "last."

Jesus had brought the dead to life; that was true. But she did not expect such a miracle. If only Andrew lived—that would be a true miracle for her.

She sat on the step by the door and stared at the midday sun contemplatively. Her life had changed so much. Not just by coming here to the Dakota Territory, but in what she found. Micah, with his compassion. Her inner strength, which had probably always been there, but buried. And most of all, the real living God, the ever-present Author of compassion.

Her eyes shut in prayer as she thanked God for all she had discovered out here, then she asked for His guidance concerning Andrew.

Her prayer was interrupted by the sound of Micah's arrival. She opened her eyes and was surprised to see that he had brought a thresher.

"Catherine, there's a storm coming. We have to hurry." The urgency in his voice was clear. "It looks bad."

"What kind of a storm?"

He brushed off her question. "We've got to move quickly or we'll lose the crop."

"I can do it." She laid her meal aside. "I'll go now."

"No, Catherine, *we* will do it. I've brought my own—"

"You don't understand," she said. "I have to do this—myself."

"Listen," he said, taking her arm, "I don't know why

you feel this need to do all of the work by yourself; however, I respect that. I wouldn't have given you a plug nickel's chance at first, but you've done it and done it alone. Now, I'm going to make this quick because we don't have time to waste. If we do this together, we can do it faster and better."

"But—" she began.

He waved away her objection. "No. Andrew and I had always planned to jointly harvest our fields, and I intend to see it through. I will not let your private battles, whatever they may be, ruin this for Andrew."

"How long do we have?"

"Probably two hours."

She didn't have time for thought. There was no choice in her decision. She must now choose for Andrew, and not for her.

And she knew her decision was right.

She nodded. "Let's do it."

As they headed out into the final section together, Catherine put her whole body and mind into the task at hand. This was her final test.

The rows had never seemed this long, nor had Orion ever moved so slowly.

She couldn't see the storm yet, but she could feel the electricity of its approach. Apparently, Orion could, too. He neighed uneasily, and she tried to calm him as she urged him on.

The mosquitoes clung to her arms and bit mercilessly, but she didn't take the time to shoo them away.

As quickly as she could, she gathered the bundles and shocked them.

Her hands were sliced and bleeding. She should have worn gloves, but going back to the house now would mean sacrificing minutes they didn't have.

Bundle after bundle. Shock after shock.

Still, she persevered. Somewhere on this expansive field Micah was working; she didn't know where. She didn't have time to lift her head and look.

She mopped the sweat from her forehead. Every muscle in her body ached. Still, she could not stop.

Tears of frustration sprang to her eyes, and she wiped them away. There was no time to cry.

But her efforts were futile.

They were losing to the storm. She knew it. The fact was as clear as the endless rows before her.

What she had left to finish would require a good four days' work. Even with their combined efforts. Even with Micah's skill. There was no way they could beat the weather that would soon bear down on them.

There was no time to stop. She prayed as she drove Orion onward. What she prayed, what syllables she used, what requests she made, she had no idea. Her prayer was a wordless petition, springing from intense need.

Oh, God. Dear God. My God. Please, God. God. God. God.

"Look!" Micah's shout called her attention to his side of the field.

From the distance, slowly but surely, more wagons,

more horses, more threshers, and more people headed for Andrew's fields.

"What are they doing?" she shouted back at him. The wind was beginning to whip up, snatching the words from her lips.

"They're your neighbors. They're coming to help."

There was no time to ask questions. The newcomers fell quickly to work, efficiently and collectively shocking the bundles, taking the bundles to the threshers now stationed around the field, and beginning the process of threshing the wheat.

She didn't know these people. Maybe they were Micah's friends, or Andrew's friends. She had no idea.

But they came, and even more followed them. Despite the gathering storm, which she could now see on the horizon, they continued to stream across the prairie, risking their own lives, and possibly their own crops, to save hers.

The field seemed to swarm with strangers and their machinery. Some had sophisticated engines that worked quickly and efficiently. Others had self-created mechanisms, similar to what Andrew and Micah had, that worked slowly but surely.

Together they toiled, each an individual but working as one.

Suddenly she realized that Micah was at her side. "Let's yoke our horses together," he shouted over the gathering wind. "We can do it even faster."

She knew he was at her side. She felt his strong

male presence, a bulwark against the storm, and she was pleased.

Together they worked the fields, until at last, as the first hailstones pelted her arms, Catherine realized that they were done.

The others were already leaving, rushing to the safety of their own homes, and she tried to thank them. But there were too many, and they were too hurried. She would have to tell them of her appreciation later.

"Unhook the horses!" Micah shouted, and Catherine automatically obeyed the command. The hailstones were coming rapidly now, larger and faster.

They ran to the barn with the horses, and from the safety of the barn, they watched the last figures on the horizon as they headed for home.

"Will they be safe?" she asked as she brushed Orion's coat. He had worked so hard that he was dripping with sweat. She had to move quickly before he got chilled.

He nodded. "The horses can take refuge under a tree—"

"A tree?" she interrupted, laughing. "Where would you find a tree here?"

He grinned in wry agreement. "Good point. There are a few, and trust me, these folks know every one. They can tie their horses under one of those trees, and they can take cover under the wagons. This isn't going to be a long storm, just a nasty one. After the storm passes, I'll go out and take care of their equipment."

"We'll go out," she corrected him, and she was

rewarded with a smile. "Who are they?"

"They're your neighbors, all good people. Most of them join together when they can to worship with us."

"Where? I don't see a church around here."

"Andrew and I were going to take part of our profits this year and build one. But that's your call now, at least until Andrew returns. We were going to break ground on it after the harvest." His voice was guarded, and he ducked his head behind his horse's broad back as he curried it.

Catherine paused and thought about his words.

Money. The crop was in and, to her eyes at least, it looked good. It should sell for a nice profit.

Initially, she'd planned to use it to bring Andrew home, to Massachusetts.

Now she couldn't imagine going back there. Her soul, in less than one month, had found its home in Dakota.

"The money should be used as Andrew wants it used. There will be hospital bills, of course, but if it is possible, yes, I would like for some of the profit to go toward building a church."

Micah's head popped up over the side of his horse, and she almost laughed at the open delight apparent in his face.

"You would, of course, be consulted until Andrew is able to make his own decisions," Micah said.

"I trust you." The words were true, and merely speaking them brought rest to her worn heart.

There was another question in Micah's eyes, one which she would have liked to answer, but it was too soon. When Andrew's condition was stabilized, when she had asked and answered all the questions in her own heart, when all was secure, then and only then would she answer.

Would he wait?

She didn't have to respond.

She trusted, and she believed. And there was no more fear.

⟨❧⟩

The sun never shines as brightly as it does after a storm, he thought while cleaning the threshers the neighbors had left. He would return them the next day when the ground had dried.

The hailstones were melting quickly in the August sun, and he pitched one across the harvested field. They'd be gone within the hour.

The birds had come out of their refuges, and the insects buzzed hungrily around his head.

All creation was back to normal.

A rainbow was poised over the horizon, a shimmering vision of God's promise.

He stopped, midaction, as he realized that the rainbow came after the rain, and not before it. There was a farmer's explanation for this: Trust in the Lord, but bring your harvest in before the storm.

God didn't want him to be foolish, just to trust Him as a working partner.

"Lord, I want a partner here on earth, someone with whom I can share my love of the land and for You. Someone who will work with me and laugh with me and worship with me. Someone who will love me and love You. Someone, dear Father, like Catherine."

Chapter 7

"Be not afraid,
only believe."
Mark 5:36

The hospital was cooler than Catherine had expected. A heat wave made the city shimmer through the tall paned windows as she and Micah walked down the long, high-ceilinged hallway toward Andrew.

Andrew, who had regained consciousness two days earlier.

Automatically, she reached for Micah's hand. It was the first time they had touched so purposely. His fingers wrapped around hers securely, and she thought she felt a slight, telltale tremble in his own hand. He was worried more than he let on.

The nurse led them onwards, her heavily starched dress moving above her feet like a white bell.

She swung sharply into a large room with four beds, two on either side.

And, at last, Catherine was at her brother's bedside.

She thought she had prepared herself for what she might see, steadied her nerves so she'd show nothing except joy, but when she saw her brother's pallid face under the snowy bandages, she crumpled against Micah.

He moved to support her, and he began to say something, but the words died on his lips when Andrew's eyes fluttered open.

"Did I miss the wedding?" Andrew's words were careful, spoken from parched lips that had difficulty forming the syllables. Immediately, the nurse was at his side, helping him take a sip of water.

Micah laughed. "Hello, Andrew."

Andrew focused on him. "I've forgotten, so you'll have to remind me again. How many children do you two have?"

Catherine smoothed the lines in his too-pale forehead. "We don't have any children. We're not married."

Her brother became agitated. "You're not getting married!"

"I didn't say that," she soothed, easing him back onto the fluffy pillow. "I didn't say that at all."

Andrew smiled. "That's good, because you belong together. I know." His words faded out, and his eyes slowly shut. He was asleep.

The nurse straightened Andrew's sheets. "He is still exhausted from this. He needs a good deal of sleep. You might as well leave. He'll sleep for a couple of hours, I suspect."

She led them back to the waiting room of St. Elizabeth's. "You are certainly welcome to stay here. If you're hungry, there's a fine eating establishment two blocks away. I'll check back here when he's awake again."

The nurse left them alone in the black-and-white-tiled room. Catherine reached into her bag and pulled out her embroidery.

"Are you hungry?" Micah asked.

She shook her head. "I couldn't eat right now."

"Me either," he agreed.

"Micah, he's so pale!" The tears she'd held back so long finally started to flow, and he took her in his arms.

"There, there," he hushed her as his work-roughened fingers stroked her hair.

"He's so thin, and so weak."

"But he's getting better," he soothed. "The doctor told us he would be back with us, probably within six weeks, perhaps a month."

"I know," she sniffled, "but I wish there were something more I could do."

"We can pray," he offered simply.

There, in the starkly tiled room, they bent their heads and silently asked the Lord to visit His presence and His healing hand upon Andrew.

Their fingers knit together, and their heads almost touched as they joined their hearts in love for her brother.

❧

The thread slipped through the cloth easily, this time pulling a golden strand as luminous as the morning sun.

"You've been working on that since we left St. Paul," Micah said. "May I see it?"

"It's not finished," she said, but she handed it to him.

"It's beautiful. 'Be not afraid, only believe.' He is going to treasure this, you know." Micah studied it. "You stitch very well. I've been watching you. You do this with a confidence that astonishes me. If I were to do this, I'd be all thumbs and toes and my thread would be knotted immediately."

She laughed as she took the sampler back from him. "I've had some practice with this. It's not unlike when I watched you start the harvest, and then I made my clumsy attempts. If you want to learn to embroider—"

"Oh, no!" He waved her offer away. "These hands are meant for horses and wheat, not for fine stitchery."

The train jolted them along, and they passed the time in friendly companionship, he reading a newspaper, she embroidering, until, at last, he laid his paper aside.

"I'm going to stretch my legs," he said, standing up. "I'll be back shortly."

He walked away, and Catherine laid the cloth she was embroidering on her lap and rubbed her eyes. She usually didn't stitch this long, and her eyes were tired.

She held her hands against her eyes, hoping the darkness would soothe the irritation.

Images began to flash before her. Andrew in the hospital bed, so waxen against the white sheets. The limpness of his hand as she touched him. The words that came so slowly and painfully from swollen lips.

She'd been taking things day by day, never looking forward and certainly never looking back.

But now, she remembered standing in Andrew's house for the first time. The cold, empty house was so clearly Andrew's, but yet, an Andrew she didn't know. She had always held tightly to their closeness. So, the sudden, awful awareness that this untamed prairie was a part of him, yet did not belong to her, staggered her.

She had moved on. Always looking forward, and never back.

Everything, everything had been for Andrew. What if the doctors were wrong? What if he never returned?

She couldn't stop the sobs that broke free from her heart. She kept her hands over her eyes and wept as though there was nothing else in the world.

She was only faintly aware that strong arms wrapped around her shoulders and gathered her in, and that a familiar voice comforted her: " 'Be not afraid. Only believe.' "

Micah.

"Ssssh, ssssh, ssssh," he said, his lips pressed against her hair. "Cry it out."

At last the tears ran themselves dry, and with one last shuddering sob, she was through. "I'm so sorry," she said to him, her voice muffled against the handkerchief he'd handed her. "I let myself succumb to weakness for a moment."

"Don't apologize. You needed to do that. I suspect you've needed to do that for a long, long time."

"Probably," she admitted, "but I hadn't intended to do so on a train."

He laughed.

The crying had made her tired, and she was glad of Micah's offer of his rolled-up coat as a pillow.

As she drifted off to sleep, she glanced out of the window and watched the landscape go by. They were still in the rolling hills of Minnesota, and she was suddenly, desperately, homesick—but not for Massachusetts. She wanted to be home—in Dakota.

Micah deposited her traveling bag inside the living room.

They were back on Andrew's claim, and she busied herself with lighting a fire to take the chill off the room.

"Brrr," she said, rubbing her arms and moving closer to the fledgling fire. "There's a special coldness in a house where no one's been. This fire should take that edge off. Come on over and warm up."

He joined her. "I was glad to see Andrew. It did my soul good to see him move, to hear him talk."

"He's so pale and so weak." Catherine cringed at the image.

"He's had a major head injury," Micah said. "It takes time."

"Well, it's that," she said, "and more. Micah, tell me the truth. Is he going to be, well, totally all right?"

"What do you mean?" Micah frowned.

"He did have a head injury, and that's where his brain is."

"Yes," he agreed.

"Will it affect his thinking?" She took a deep breath

and blurted it out. "He speaks so slowly and he seems, well, confused. Micah, he doesn't seem to be quite right in his mind."

"Because he said we were getting married?" Micah's voice was only a whisper in her ear.

She pulled away and wiped furiously at her eyes. "Oh, Micah, I've known about that all along. It was a foolish idea he had and—"

The sudden hurt in Micah's eyes told her everything she had wanted to know.

"Micah," she said gently, touching his face, "is it really what you want? Please tell me."

He took her hand from his cheek and held it tightly. "From the first time Andrew spoke about you, I began to imagine what you must be like. And from that grew a dream, a foolish dream, that someday you might be my wife."

Foolish dream? Catherine's heart suspended beating. It was as she had feared—he didn't want her after all.

"But then," he continued, "you came out here, and I realized that my dream had been just that—a dream— but you were real, flesh and blood."

"You didn't want me." There. She had said the words he was afraid to say. He began to speak, but she waved his words away. "No, no. I know I'm no beauty. You can't hurt me with that. I know it's a fact."

"That's not it at all." He held her hand even tighter. "You were better and so perfect, that I had to abandon the dream. And I realized that you wouldn't want to stay here with me, a wheat farmer in Dakota. . . ."

Her heart began to beat again.

"What are your plans when your brother comes home?" he asked, his voice husky.

She hadn't planned on it being this way. She had wanted to tell him in her own way, in her own time, once she had figured it all out herself.

But she went to her bag and took out the sampler. "It's done," she said, and she handed it to him.

He didn't speak, and for a moment she was afraid he didn't understand what she was trying to say.

"Does this mean—?" His chocolate-drop eyes asked her the question, too.

She ran her finger along the edge. "I added this on the way home."

There was a new border. An amber wheat field in full grain against a vivid Dakota sunset ran around the edge.

"You did all this on the way home?"

"It goes quickly when the heart is in it."

"It means—?"

"It means I think I will stay. Andrew will need me."

"Yes, he will," Micah agreed.

It seemed as if neither one of them breathed for a long while.

Then, at last, Micah broke the silence. "You answered that question. Will you answer another?"

It was moving so quickly, this thing that she had wanted and was yet so afraid of.

She bent her head and could not speak.

He spoke for her. "Catherine, I know this is very sudden, but would you consider being my wife?"

Her heart answered first.

"Yes, Micah, I will—consider it. I cannot agree to marry you until Andrew is back and healthy once again. If, by the time a year has come and gone, another crop planted and harvested, you still want me and I still want you, then, yes. I will marry you."

"Walk with me in the moonlight," Micah said suddenly.

They went as one into the fields, now cleared of grain. The harvest was in, but the greatest one was yet to come. There was no reason for fear, only belief, for those who loved each other and their Lord.

The prairie was warm that night, and the sky was aglow with starlight. He could feel it, so clearly: All creation was happy.

His prayer was simple and heartfelt. "Thank You for the chance to love. It is enough."

Epilogue

"Be not afraid, only believe."
Mark 5:36

They walked down the road together. They were going slowly because the little boy alternately begged to be carried and to be allowed to walk on his own. A soft July breeze sent a strand of the woman's hair across her face, and the man smoothed it back behind her ear.

The church's bell began to toll, the call to worship ringing across the prairie, and the three hastened their footsteps.

"We don't want to be late, Cooper," Catherine said to her son.

He looked at her with eyes as dark as his father's. "No. Up." His chubby arms were lifted to her, and she swung him up to balance him on her waist. She never tired of this, nor did he.

Micah looked at his wife and child, and his heart flooded with warmth. Four years ago, he had prayed for love, and now he had it not once, but twofold.

A man could not be happier, he thought.

A shout from the converging road told them that Andrew and his new wife, Ardette, were late this morning, too.

Catherine's brother now walked without any hesitation at all. The only sign of his injury was a faint scar along his hairline.

The five walked to church together, hurrying their footsteps to arrive before the first hymn began.

As she slid into the pew next to her husband, their son nestled between them, half on her lap and half on his, she let herself look at the picture on the wall beside the altar.

There, bordered by a frame that Andrew had carved during his rehabilitation, was her stitchery. The letters caught the gentle Sunday sunshine and seemed to glow with the message: "Be not afraid, only believe."

She realized that Micah was watching her, and she smiled.

There was no fear in her heart; there was only love, for now she believed.

JANET SPAETH
Janet figures she has it all, living between the prairies of North Dakota and the north woods of Minnesota. She has been blessed with the "world's best family." From tallest to shortest, they are husband Kevin, daughter Megan, son Nick, and cat Quicksilver. Janet is honored to write stories that reflect the happiness of love guided by God.

A Letter to Our Readers

Dear Readers:

In order that we might better contribute to your reading enjoyment, we would appreciate you taking a few minutes to respond to the following questions. When completed, please return to the following: Fiction Editor, Barbour Publishing, Inc., P.O. Box 719, Uhrichsville, OH 44683.

1. Did you enjoy reading *Harvest Home?*
   □ Very much. I would like to see more books like this.
   □ Moderately—I would have enjoyed it more if _____
   _____
   _____

2. What influenced your decision to purchase this book?
   (Check those that apply.)
   □ Cover   □ Back cover copy   □ Title   □ Price
   □ Friends   □ Publicity   □ Other

3. Which story was your favorite?
   □ *Harvest of Love*   □ *Sunshine Harvest*
   □ *The Applesauce War*   □ *Only Believe*

4. Please check your age range:
   □ Under 18   □ 18–24   □ 25–34
   □ 35–45   □ 46–55   □ Over 55

5. How many hours per week do you read? _____

Name _____

Occupation _____

Address _____

City _____ State _____ Zip _____